HOW TO RETU

In this Series

Other titles in preparation

RETURN TO
WORK

Building new skills, new confidence and a new career

Ann Dobson

How To Books

Other titles by the same author

How to Communicate at Work
How to Write Business Letters

British Library Cataloguing in Publication Data
A catalogue record for this book is available from the British Library.

© Copyright 1995 by Ann Dobson.

First published in 1995 by How To Books Ltd, Plymbridge House, Estover
Road, Plymouth PL6 7PZ, United Kingdom. Tel: Plymouth (01752) 735251/
695745. Fax: (01752) 695699. Telex: 45635.

Note: The material contained in this book is set out in good faith for general
guidance and no liability can be accepted for loss or expense incurred as a
result of relying in particular circumstances on statements made in the book.
The law and regulations are complex and liable to change, and readers should
check the current position with the relevant authorities before making
personal arrangements.

Typeset by Concept Communications (Design & Print) Ltd, Crayford, Kent.
Printed and bound by The Cromwell Press, Broughton Gifford, Melksham,
Wiltshire.

Contents

List of Illustrations

Preface

An increasing number of people, both men and women, are returning to work after a career break. There are a number of reasons why people take such a break. The most familiar reason is to bring up a family, but looking after a dependent relative, returning home from abroad, or beginning a new life after a spell in prison could also mean a return to the work environment.

Returning to work is never easy. Technology changes, people change and your own ideas might have changed too. It is very important to make the right decisions, taking your time to decide on a suitable job which will give you some degree of satisfaction. That might mean returning to a similar type of job to the one you had before your break, or taking the opportunity to try something completely new.

Like most things worth having in life, returning to work takes effort, self-discipline and, above all, a belief in your own ability to succeed. You need to know where to look for a job and how to project yourself at an interview. You may have to master new technology, take on responsibility, and/or cope with a family who don't want you to work anyway. Perhaps you will decide to work for yourself rather than for others which, far from being an easy option, takes just as much careful planning and self-discipline as working for someone else.

The aim of this book is to make your return to work a worthwhile and stimulating experience rather than a badly-organised nightmare.

Ann Dobson

1
Why Return to Work at All?

CONSIDERING THE FACTS

At the time of writing, jobs are not in plentiful supply. However what is reassuring to those of you planning to **return to work** is that the odds are stacked heavily in favour of you being offered what is available. This is due to two facts. Firstly, as a result of a fall in the birthrate during the '60s and '70s, there are at present fewer young people seeking employment. Secondly, there is a growing realisation among employers that a mature person is usually more reliable and more committed than a young person.

Employers are, it would seem, actively seeking returners to work, often stating 'mature person preferred' in job advertisements. Some employers will even go out of their way to make provision for mothers with children, giving them time off in the school holidays, creche facilities and shorter working hours, although it must be said that such employers are still in the minority.

It should also be borne in mind that **self employment** may be an attractive option, either through necessity if you are not able to find a suitable employed position, or through choice. Working in your own business may seem particularly attractive if you dislike being told what to do by someone else and want to be in charge of your own destiny. Assuming that you genuinely feel you have a good plan for a business of your own, then do some research and consider putting your plan into action.

Reasons for taking a break

Most people will have taken a break from work because of a change in their circumstances. For instance, you may have left your job:

- to become a mother and look after your children
- to become a house husband looking after the children while your partner works

Are you:

A housewife?   A house husband

A mother with children at home?

A carer?   Returning from a spell abroad?

An ex convict?

An early retirer?   Recovering from illness?

A redundant worker?

Long term unemployed?   An ex member of the Armed Forces?

Are you feeling:

Hard up?   Frustrated?   Shy?

Bored?   Lacking purpose?   Moody?

Disappointed?   Disheartened?   Unimportant?

At a loss?   Unhappy?   Worthless?

Unloved?   Rejected?   'Outside' the real world?

If so, returning to work could make you:

Happy   Contented   Richer

Confident   Fulfilled   Needed

Secure   Positive   Satisfied

Independent   Poised   Part of society

Fig. 1. Is this you?

- because your other half was earning sufficient for you to stay at home and the idea seemed attractive to you
- due to an illness
- to care for a dependent relative
- to work abroad for a period of time
- because you had to go to prison.

You might want to return to work for a variety of different reasons too and these are looked at in greater detail below. Do bear in mind though that whatever your particular reason for wanting to return to work, you stand as good a chance as everyone else in the job market of today — some would say an even better chance because of your maturity. Never think of your maturity as a handicap.

NEEDING THE MONEY

Many, many people who return to work do so because they need the money. In fact, to take that statement one stage further, the vast majority of all workers go to work largely to earn money. We need money for almost everything, and whilst health and happiness should always come first in our list of priorities, money comes a very close second.

This is not to say, of course, that job satisfaction and a genuine interest in what you do are not important too. It is possible both to earn money and enjoy your working life. This is the ideal situation and the goal to aim for when returning to work.

True job satisfaction is much easier to achieve if you are able to spend time choosing the type of job you want to do. This might involve re-training, or taking a refresher course, delaying the moment of receiving your first 'earnings', but in the long term your earning capacity could be far greater than if you take the first job that comes along, Try not to let your need to earn money work against your better judgement. Unless you are absolutely on the bread-line think about your prospects on a long term, rather than a short term, basis.

EARNING SELF RESPECT

The dictionary definition of self respect is 'proper regard for oneself and one's own dignity and principles etc'. Of course, you may feel you possess a good measure of self respect and certainly do not need to earn it. You may be perfectly content at home all day, love every minute of your family life, and have no wish to return to work in any shape or form. However, if you feel that way you would presumably not be reading this book. The fact that you are suggests that you could do with boosting your ego at least just a little bit.

If you have spent several years looking after a dependent relative, for instance, you will probably have had no time for a social life or to think about yourself and your beliefs and ambitions. You may feel that you can no longer contribute to the outside working world, and your self respect will probably be at an all-time low.

Certainly life at home with children can also make you think that you will never count for anything in the outside world again. You may wonder if there is any boss anywhere who would be willing to take you on with ten years of child caring experience as your only recent achievement.

By returning to work you will be able to prove to yourself as well as to everyone around you that you really can change your life, broaden your horizons and re-discover your self respect at the same time. And, if you happen to be a parent, don't ever feel that you are compromising that special bond with your family. By believing in yourself, you will probably become a better mother or father too!

GIVING YOURSELF AN INTEREST

It is very important for every one of us to have an interest or purpose in life outside our family unit.

Maybe you think you already have an interest. Perhaps you enjoy gardening, or golf, belong to a drama club or love to cook. But how about taking on an interest that you will get paid for? After all if you decide to return to work, not only will you be providing yourself with a new interest but you will also be earning money at the same time. That must make good sense!

The interest factor obviously depends on the type of work you return to — some jobs are far more interesting than others, but even a boring job will mean new people to talk to, new skills to acquire and new things to think about, and extra money as well.

Fortunately for employers, and for ourselves too, we all find different types of work interesting. One person might love digging roads, leaping out of bed each morning eager and willing to start a new day. Another person might enjoy working with a computer, finding the machine fascinating and the work stimulating. Yet a third person might hate both possibilities and prefer to work in a shop. Any job can be interesting if the person finds it to be so. What you need to think about is exactly what job not only sounds interesting but is also a practical choice for you to consider.

ENJOYING THE CHALLENGE

Everyone sets themselves various challenges in their lives, certain goals they want to achieve. It should be remembered, however, that what is a challenge to one person could be a nightmare to another. Like interests, challenges are based on personal choices.

Returning to work can prove to be an enjoyable and stimulating challenge, provided enough planning and forethought are given to all the factors involved before deciding on how great or small that challenge should be.

It is very important to make sure that the challenge you intend to take on is a realistic one. There is no point, for instance, in considering a job which involves working every evening from 6 pm to midnight, if you know your partner has to go out on business several evenings a week, often at short notice, making it difficult to find a babysitter.

Similarly, a job involving heavy lifting, although it might appeal to you, could be disastrous if you have a 'dodgy back' that can let you down at any time. These sort of challenges you can well do without!

COPING WITH CHILDREN BECOMING INDEPENDENT

Are you a mother who suddenly feels unwanted and unloved? Have your children matured, all of a sudden, into young adults, who seem to need you only to provide them with food, clean clothes, and money? This can, of course, equally apply to house husband fathers too, but men tend to be less emotional about such things.

If you have been a devoted mother, always there to cope with life's little emergencies, running your offspring here, there and everywhere to their various activities, then the realisation that they no longer need you will come as a very big shock.

Once you get over feeling sorry for yourself, however, that shock may well be replaced by feelings of boredom, frustration and sheer loneliness. Although you have things to do at home, those household chores no longer hold much appeal (if they ever did). Six, eight or even ten hours of peace and quiet might seem like bliss to a young mother tearing her hair out with toddlers running everywhere, but to you those hours may drag until you almost start talking to the television for company.

Going back to work, either for yourself or for someone else, can prove to be a very good solution to such a problem. Don't be surprised though if you encounter opposition from your offspring. They might not actually need you any more, but they still like the services you provide. Hard though it may be, you must point out that you have put them first for long enough, and now it is time for you to show some independence too.

CASE STUDIES

Throughout the book six people will be used as case studies to illustrate the points made in each chapter. Their names and backgrounds are described below.

Sue

Sue is 35. She is divorced and has two children aged five and twelve. She needs to go back to work to earn some money. Now that both children are at school she is looking for a job within school hours. Sue is quite reluctant to go back to work at all and doesn't think she is capable of much. She used to work in an office as a clerk. She resents the position her ex-husband has left her in — he cannot afford to pay her much maintenance as he is unemployed.

Paula

Paula is 40. She is married with one son aged two. Paula and her husband do not need the money (he is a doctor), but she cannot stand being at home. She is arranging for a nanny to look after the child and intends to return to full-time work. She worked as a nurse before giving birth to her son, but does not want to return to nursing.

John

John is 30. He lives with his partner and their two children aged five and six. He trained as a teacher but he and his partner decided on a role reversal for a few years as her earning potential was far higher than his. Now the two children are at school he intends to return to some form of work. He feels he would like to try self employment but is not sure whether he would be sufficiently self disciplined to work for himself.

Mary

Mary is 52. She worked for many years in a family shop, but left when she was 40 to look after her elderly mother. Now her mother has died and Mary wants to go back to doing a job of some sort. She thinks she will go back to shop work if she can, but feels her age is against her. She is desperately lonely. Her own children are married and although she has a husband, he is very wrapped up in his own life.

Richard

Richard is 28. He has been in prison for five years for drug offences, but he does not intend getting involved with drugs ever again. He has a girlfriend and she has been bringing up their six year old daughter. He is now determined to prove to them as well as himself that he can go straight and get a worthwhile job. The only work he has ever done in the past is lorry driving.

Andrew

Andrew is 43. He has spent many years travelling the world, trying various different jobs and never sticking at any one for very long. He has a degree but has never put it to good use, being more intent on having a good time. He has now met the 'love of his life' and wants to settle down with her in England. He is not sure what he wants to do, but feels that some sort of office work would probably be the most respectable option to choose.

CHECKLIST

- Are you really serious about wanting to return to work?

- Have you thought about what you want to do?

- Are you returning to work just to earn extra money?

- Are you looking for something interesting and challenging?

- Have you lost your self-respect?

- Does your ego need a boost?

- Have your children become independent?

- Do you think that your family as well as yourself will benefit if you return to work?

POINTS FOR DISCUSSION

1   Make a list of all the jobs you would like to do. Study the list carefully, crossing off any that you know are not a feasible proposition for you, because of the hours, the pay, the training, lack of availability etc. Keep the remaining choices on one side to consider one by one as you read each chapter of the book.

2   Do you think that returning to work can be harder than starting for the first time? If so, why? Do you think your age, assuming you are between 30 and 40, will work in your favour or against you?

3   If one job is well paid but boring and another is interesting but doesn't pay so much, which one would you go for, assuming you are really hard up? Bear in mind when making your decision that you hope to be back at work for 20 years or so.

2
Deciding on the Right Sort of Job

WORKING FOR YOURSELF OR SOMEONE ELSE?

The very first decision to make when returning to work is whether to work for yourself or someone else.

Every year, thousands upon thousands of people start their own business, but only a small handful succeed beyond the first year or so. Many of the failures are due to lack of research into whether or not the business idea is a viable one, to lack of start-up capital, or to a mistaken assessment of the individual's capabilities.

Working for yourself should never be seen as a soft option. On the other hand, setting up a properly thought out and managed business venture can provide tremendous rewards, both financially and in terms of self satisfaction. Specific points relating to self employment are discussed in more detail in Chapters 10 and 11.

CHOOSING BETWEEN PERMANENT AND TEMPORARY WORK

If you opt to work for someone else, you will then need to decide between permanent or temporary work.

Permanent work
The traditional way of working is to work for one employer as a permanent member of staff, either on a full or part time basis, enjoying all the security and benefits that are available to you.

Advantages of permanent work

- Job security.
- Paid-for sick leave and holidays.

- More chance of part-time work.
- Usually prospects for promotion.
- More responsibility than in most temporary jobs.
- A regular income allowing you to budget.

Disadvantages of permanent work

- Could be a false sense of security if staff cuts have to be made and you lose your job.
- Problems if children are ill, or you cannot go to work for some reason.
- Same job may become repetitive after a while.
- May be asked to take on too much responsibility too soon.

Temporary work

Most people think of temporary work in terms of working for an employment agency and going on different assignments each week. Increasingly, however, organisations are taking on temporary staff direct, often on a fixed-term basis. This suits employers who are unsure of their staffing levels in the present economic climate, or do not like paying exorbitant agency fees.

Advantages of temporary work

- No long term commitment on your part.
- Flexible working hours.
- Variety of work.
- Good way to gain experience.
- Can lead to suitable permanent work at a later date.

Disadvantages of temporary work

- No long-term job security.
- Can be made to feel that you do not fit in with the permanent staff.
- Difficult to cope with if you are naturally shy and are frequently changing jobs.
- Often given the jobs that no one else wants to do.
- May not receive holiday or sickness pay.
- Not a regular income.

WOULD PERMANENT OR TEMPORARY WORK BE BEST?

Do you need job security?	Yes	No
Can you guarantee cover for your family?	Yes	No
Do you have relevant experience?	Yes	No
Do you like to work with the same people?	Yes	No
Are you looking for responsibility?	Yes	No
Do you want to be in line for promotion?	Yes	No
Do you want to work part time hours?	Yes	No
Do you see your job as a long term move?	Yes	No
Do you need a regular income?	Yes	No

Fig. 2. Permanent or temporary?

If you have answered 'yes' to at least six of these questions then permanent work would be the best choice for you. Otherwise, try temporary work to begin with until you feel more settled in life generally.

DECIDING ON THE HOURS

Working out what hours you can devote to your working life involves more than just deciding between full or part time work. You have to decide whether you are prepared to work at weekends, during the evening or sometimes right through the night. It may be possible to **job share**, which is a way of working where two or more people share one full-time job between them, or you may be able to work **flexitime**, where the total number of hours you work is fixed, but you can choose, within reason, when you work them. Different jobs have different requirements and it is very important to consider your family situation when making that decision.

It seems that as each year goes by, more and more people are being asked to work **unsociable hours**. As we, the public, demand more and more shopping facilities, for instance, so workers have to be employed to satisfy that need. Shift workers are no longer confined to manufacturing industry, nursing, the police and other traditional 'out of hours' occupations. Sometimes, although not always, unsociable working hours are rewarded with higher pay. This might compensate for the inconvenience caused, and in some cases evening or weekend work is more suitable than a normal daytime job. A mother with children might be able to fit these hours in around her partner's working life. For instance, many of the new superstores employ women who will happily work every Sunday for some extra money. When jobs are scarce, you may have to reach a compromise over the hours you are asked to work. Do not however, let the prospect of earning good money persuade you to take on a job that you know you will never be able to manage without completely reorganising the lives of everyone around you. That will not make your return to work an enjoyable experience at all! The same principles apply to self employment too, where the temptation is often greater to work long hours, leaving no time to spend with family and friends.

WHAT RESPONSIBILITIES CAN YOU COPE WITH?

You will, no doubt, be familiar with the saying 'Never try to run before you can walk'. This is very apt when applied to returning to work.

If you held a responsible position before your break, there is a chance that you will be able to step straight back into a similar position. What is more likely, however, is that you will be expected to start a little further down the ladder when you first return to work. This could well be to your benefit as jobs change over the years and you will probably need time to adjust to those changes.

Try not to resent a younger person who is now doing the same kind of job as you did before your break. You might feel that you would be far better at it, but remember that he or she will have up-to-date training and experience. It will take you some time to regain your previous skills and learn the necessary new ones. You can afford to bide your time. After all, your new life has only just started!

Those of you considering a completely different type of job will definitely need to start at the bottom and work up. Age and maturity, assets though they may be, still need to be coupled with relevant experience.

We have assumed so far that you will not be taking on too much responsibility immediately you return to work. This is obviously not true in every case. For instance, a general practitioner returning to work after a break will be treating patients from day one in much the same way as before. Presumably, however, he or she will have accepted this fact before returning.

If you are just thinking about returning to work and how much responsibility you can take on, always err on the side of caution to begin with. If this will be your first experience of work for a long time, it is far better to learn all about the job first, and then increase the level of responsibility afterwards. That way you should never feel panicked or unable to cope.

RETURNING TO THE FAMILIAR OR TRYING SOMETHING NEW?

Did you enjoy your job when you were last employed, or did the thought of going to work each day fill you with dread? This is the first question to ask yourself when deciding what job to consider when returning to work.

Obviously, if you were very happy before and your job still exists, then there is much to be said for returning to the same type of work. If you were specially trained, for instance as a teacher, then those skills can be put back into action. Admittedly you will need to do some research on how teaching methods and expectations have changed over the years, but hopefully you will have kept yourself broadly up to date with the various changes in education.

Unfortunately, there is the possibility that even if you want to return to your old work it may no longer exist and you will be forced to think about trying something new. Or, as we said before, you may have intensely disliked your previous work, in which case you will definitely want to think about a change in direction.

With all the training opportunities available for mature students, and the increased possibilities of self employment too, it is never too late to take on something completely new. To start with though, you must give some thought to what you would like to do. Retraining is discussed in more detail in Chapter 3.

CONSIDERING THE FAMILY

A single person, with no family ties or partner, will only have them-selves to consider when deciding to work. Such people are, however, in the minority. Most of us do have someone else to think about, and that person or persons should definitely be taken into consideration when working out what job would be the best one to go for.

A mother with young children has to think about school holidays, children's sickness and what will happen to them after school if she is working full time. A house husband will need to think about the same things when he decides to go back to work. A man with a partner who relies on him to be there in the evenings and weekends, should give careful thought to the offer of a sales job involving extensive travel abroad.

Considering the family really is important. Without the support of those around you, your return to the workplace will be very hard to cope with. If your home life is stable and happy, your working life is likely to be too. Constant harassment and resentment at home will mean you will feel too tired and fraught to give proper attention to your job, and if you are not able to do that job well, then you might find yourself replaced by someone who can. Similarly, starting out in self employ-ment will be extremely difficult without your family's cooperation.

If you have a partner, talk to him or her about your intentions, **before** deciding what you are going to do. Talking over various possibilities and discussing the pros and cons can help you to come to a decision on your future which suits not only you, but also those you care about. After all, 'a problem shared is a problem halved'.

If you have children who will be affected by you going back to work, discuss the situation with them too. Make them feel that they will still be loved just as much, and that the extra money could help to pay for special treats or that trip to Euro Disney. Bribery works wonders!

CASE STUDIES

Sue

Sue, as we already know, needs to find a job where she can work school hours only. She thinks that temporary work would be her best choice, so that she is not tied down to regular employment. She is particularly worried about what will happen when the children are ill as she has no one to look after them. She feels that if she takes a permanent job she will be letting her employer down if she needs to take time off.

Sue does not want to take on too much responsibility and only wants to do a basic clerical job. Her aim is to earn money and that is the only reason she is returning to work. Her satisfaction in life comes from her children. She is devoted to them and has no intention of becoming involved with a man again.

Paula

Paula, in complete contrast to Sue, wants a permanent job with lots of responsibility and interest. Although she loves her husband and son, she feels she has given up five years of her life and now intends to make up that lost time. Before her son was born she suffered three miscarriages and her husband more or less forced her to give up work as he desperately wanted her to have a child. She considers she has done her duty and now has every intention of putting her own life first.

Having arranged child care for her son, Paula's only problem is deciding what kind of job to look for. She does not want to return to nursing which is all she is really trained to do. Her aim is to find a new career rather than just a job.

John

John intends to take one step at a time. He really wants to try self employment and is thinking of setting up a small training school, offering courses in English for foreign students. He thinks he can easily work this type of business around the school holidays when he will be responsible for looking after the children once more.

The main problem for John is that his partner will have to put up some of the money to get him started and he feels this takes some thinking about.

Mary

Mary has lost all her self confidence. Because she has looked after her mother for so long she now feels she has no future at all. She would like to find a permanent part-time job in a shop, giving her somewhere to belong and people to talk to.

Her husband works long hours in his own business. Over the years he has had to make his own life while his wife spent so much time with her mother. Now they are both finding it hard to come to terms with the changed circumstances. He thinks it will be good for Mary to get a job. He also knows that they will both have to work hard to make time for each other and become close again.

Richard

Whilst in prison, Richard received a good deal of advice from the prison officers and the probation service. He is now determined to get back to work as soon as possible, although he is not sure what that work will be.

Prison was a big shock to Richard. He never felt he belonged there and worked as hard as he could to prove to himself and everyone else that he was determined to reform. He attended various training courses and particularly enjoyed working with computers.

Richard feels he will be lucky to get any job at all, so he thinks he will keep an open mind and see what comes along. He feels genuinely sorry for the trouble he has caused his girlfriend and for the years he has missed with her and their daughter. He just wants to show them that he can do well now as a thank you to them for waiting for him.

Andrew

Andrew just doesn't know where to start in his search for work. He finds it very difficult to focus his thoughts on any sort of permanent employment as he has spent so many years flitting from place to place and job to job. Although he feels he ought to be looking for office work, he is not sure if he could stand being confined to one place all day. He wonders whether to train for something new. Responsibility worries him too. He wants respectability with no hassle attached.

CHECKLIST

- Do you want to work for yourself or someone else?
- Should you be looking for permanent or temporary work?
- Can you work full-time or only part-time?

- How much responsibility can you cope with?
- Would you like to return to your old job?
- Does your old job still exist?
- How about trying something new?
- Have you any ideas of what that new job could be?
- Are you considering the family as well as yourself?
- Have you spoken to them about your intentions?

POINTS FOR DISCUSSION

1 Write out exactly what form you want your job to take in terms of permanent or temporary, hours of work, responsibility, location, etc. Keep this with you whenever you consider any jobs and make sure you do not compromise too much on your ideals.

2 Do you think Paula (see Case Studies) is selfish in wanting to return to work with such a young son? State the reasons for your answer and what you think she should do if her husband still wants her to stay at home.

3 When someone leaves prison, do you think they should be given more or less help than the rest of the population to enable them to find employment? Give your reasons.

3
Getting up to Date

RETRAINING POSSIBILITIES

Having decided on the type of work which interests you, it is very possible that you will want either to up-date your current skills or to train for something completely new.

There are a number of government schemes all aimed to help those who want to work. These include:

- **Training for Work** — This has replaced Employment Training and is available to those who have been unemployed for six months. It is also available to 'Labour market returners' who can gain immediate entry to the scheme. (Labour market returners are people returning to work who have not been claiming any benefit.) Training for Work offers work placements and also college courses where the aim is to update or learn new skills leading to recognised qualifications such as NVQs (National Vocational Qualifications). Those claiming benefit are paid while they train, plus an extra £10 a week.

- **Business Start Up Scheme** — This scheme is available for those who want to become self employed. Various short courses give advice on how to set up your business, and government funding of £1,000 is paid over a 40 week period (£30 for first 20 weeks, £20 for next 20 weeks). In order to qualify you must have been out of work for six weeks (but not necessarily claiming benefit), have at least £1,000 to invest and be starting a new rather than an existing business.

- **Career Development Loans** — As a result of a partnership arrangement between the Employment Department and certain banks, you may be able to borrow the money for a course of training and then pay it back after your training has finished. This is particularly useful if you are not able to train under the **Training for Work** scheme because you are not eligible or the course you wish to take is not eligible. You can borrow up to 80% of the course fees, plus books, materials and other expenses, and you may also be able to borrow money to help with your living expenses. While you train the Employment Department pay the interest on your loan; you take over the loan and interest three months after your training ceases.

It is possible that you may be able to obtain a grant for a course at a college or university from your local education authority.

Places to retrain

Universities and Polytechnics
Have you longed to go to university but never had the chance until now? Or would you like to take a specialised course at a polytechnic? It is never too late to acquire a degree, and you will be taken very seriously in the workplace if you have achieved your degree as a mature student.

Open University
You can take an Open University degree by studying at home. This can be quite expensive to finance but is very worthwhile if you are not in too much of a hurry to return to work. Credits are gained over a period of around 5-6 years and the final degree is considered to be of equal status to that gained during a traditional university course.

Further education colleges
Increasing numbers of courses are offered by further education colleges. The list of subjects is extensive and many courses lead to diplomas and certificates.

Private colleges
A number of private colleges offer specialised courses in many subjects. These courses, although they are not usually government funded, can offer training at a far brisker pace than at a further education college. This is because numbers tend to be smaller so more attention can be given to each individual.

On the job training
As well as the government funded work placements, many companies and organisations are willing to train their own personnel. Usually lower wages are paid until the training is completed.

CONTACTING THE RIGHT PEOPLE

It is very important to find out who to contact about opportunities in your particular area.

Jobcentres
These are to be found in most towns and cities. They offer not only advice on available jobs, but they can also point you in the right direction for retraining, and will give you all the information you need on current government schemes.

Training and Enterprise Councils/Local Enterprise Companies (TECs and LECs)
These are independent bodies led by local business people in partnership with the public and voluntary sectors. They give information and advice on training and are responsible for the government training programmes discussed above.

Careers offices
Careers offices have developed over the last few years. They are called different names in different parts of the country. They aim to give career advice to everyone, whatever their age. They offer special counselling sessions to help people make the right decision as far as their choice of job is concerned.

Universities and polytechnics
Approach the university or polytechnic of your choice and enquire about entry qualifications and the courses on offer.

Further education colleges
Your local college will send you full literature on any courses which are of interest to you. If you are not quite clear about the content of a particular course, or whether your qualifications are adequate, make an appointment to see the head of the relevant department. Most further education colleges are staffed by friendly people who are only too ready to give advice.

Open University and private colleges
The address for the Open University is given later in this book. If you write to them they will send you full information on all their courses.

Similarly, most private colleges will gladly send you a prospectus if you give them a ring.

Private employment agencies
Many employment agencies offer their own training courses, particularly for computer work. If agencies train their own staff and then send them out on working assignments, they know the standard of the people they are employing. Such agencies may also prove to be a useful way of finding out about employment trends generally.

ATTENDING A COLLEGE COURSE

Beginning a course at a large college or university can prove rather daunting to the more mature person, but colleges and universities are not just for the young. Over the last few years, colleges of further education in particular have begun to cater more and more for the returner to work, and many different courses are geared specifically to mature students. So when you start your course you will probably not be anywhere near the oldest student there.

One point that is worth mentioning, however, concerns clothes. Whatever their age, students tend to dress in a casual way. There is no need for you to lower your standards as far as cleanliness and smartness are concerned, but do not overdress or you will feel uncomfortable. Suits, either for men or women, are not generally worn! Use your initiative, wear something smart but casual for the first day, and then take your lead from the others.

Speaking from personal experience, the refectory at lunchtime can be rather daunting too. Unless you are the type who can converse with anyone of any age and in any situation, you might prefer to take some sandwiches and try to slip out each day for a walk, at least for the first week or so.

Even the strangest looking students can turn out to be very friendly underneath (perhaps you know one of them as your own son or daughter), so never be afraid to ask someone the way if you get lost, or just smile and look friendly as you pass in the corridor. The more you enter into the spirit of university or college life the more you will enjoy your time there.

Private colleges are rather different. They are usually much smaller than state colleges and many mature students are attracted to them for that reason alone. Classes tend to be smaller too, and usually everyone forms a common bond very quickly. Individual help can be given if you

Life as a mature student - do's and don'ts

Do

- Dress casually and comfortably

- Look friendly and approachable

- Involve yourself a little in the social life

- Keep up with assignments

- Ask for help if you have a problem

- Discuss course work with other students

- Make the most of opportunities offered.

Don't

- Wear a suit

- Borrow your daughter's clothes

- Say 'when I was your age'

- Be outspokenly disapproving

- Act 20 years younger than you are

- Party all night

- Force yourself into situations where you feel uncomfortable

- Try to cope with too much

Fig.3. Coping with life as a mature student.

have a particular problem and often flexible hours are arranged to work around children and other commitments.

Both state and private colleges offer evening classes in various subjects. It obviously takes longer to learn by just attending college for one or two evenings each week, but sometimes this can be a good way of getting up to date in advance of going back to work, particularly for young mothers, who may be still tied down during the day.

WATCHING TV PROGRAMMES

You may be wondering how watching television helps you to get up to date with skills and attributes for particular jobs. It is true that the average 'soap' is unlikely to give you much inspiration, but many other television programmes may prove to be very useful to you.

Try watching some of the excellent factual programmes, for instance. Many of them nowadays deal with the workplace in various different forms. Some outline the successes and failures of the self employed, others may show different companies along with their associated jobs and what these involve.

During the day there are special programmes aimed at schools and colleges. These too can provide a wealth of information on training and employment possibilities.

Be selective in your viewing. Look at the television listings at the beginning of the week and mark those programmes that you think will be of particular interest to you, both for viewing pleasure and for furthering your knowledge of a particular subject. It is just possible that an episode of 'Eastenders' or 'Coronation Street' will give you an insight into a job you had not even thought of!

READING RELEVANT BOOKS

Generally speaking, those who regularly read books tend to be the most interesting people to be with. Along with newspapers, books provide us with a wealth of information on every conceivable subject.

If you have access to a public library then there is nowhere better to go to find any book you need. Most libraries have a computerised system whereby you can look up what you want by author, title or subject. If your branch does not stock the book you want it can then be ordered from another branch.

Several careers books have been written in recent years which list hundreds of different job possibilities. There are also books giving specific jobs suitable for the more mature and whole books devoted to just one job possibility. (See the list of other titles in the 'How To' series for some ideas.) Any of these careers books will give you an idea of what is available and what qualifications you will need. In addition, reference libraries usually hold books telling you which courses are offered where, if you have something specialised in mind.

Reading general books, both fiction and non-fiction, will improve your knowledge of what goes on around you. Read what you enjoy and what interests you. You never know when your newly acquired information will come in useful. If nothing else, you will be able to list reading as one of your interests on your CV!

CASE STUDIES

Sue

Sue decides to approach an agency. She tells them that she is looking for temporary clerical work and they ask her what her skills consist of. She says she can type accurately, but has not used a word processor. The agency tell her that they will not be able to find her anything at all unless she can use the WordPerfect word processing package, as this is what most of the local businesses are using now.

The agency are not able to offer her any training, so although she is on a limited budget, Sue decides to contact a local private secretarial college. They arrange a six week course for her, to include an examination at the end.

Within two months of her original visit, Sue returns to the agency, and is welcomed with a far more positive attitude from the lady who interviewed her before. She is given a typing and word processing test and does so well that she is immediately added to their list of reliable employees.

Paula

Paula thinks she has had a marvellous idea. She has decided to investigate the possibility of opening a small residential nursing home, aimed at short stay patients recovering from operations and illnesses. With her nursing background and her husband on hand too, she feels this will be a really exciting venture. She longs to be her own boss and has already started looking around for suitable properties Her husband does not yet share her enthusiasm for the project and will take a lot of convincing before he parts with any of their money to set this up.

Paula sees no need to get involved in the Business Start Up Scheme.

She thinks that this is aimed at those with no business sense, and that she knows exactly how to go about it all.

John

John has heard about the Business Start Up Scheme and, unlike Paula, thinks it sounds a good idea, so he contacts his local Jobcentre to find out more about it. They arrange some training sessions for him. These are designed to help someone who is thinking about setting up in business and John finds them very useful. He hopes he will meet the criteria for the weekly payment under the Scheme for the first 40 weeks (see page 28), as he feels that this will make him less dependent on his partner's money, even if she does help him financially to set up the business. He is told that his business could be an official partnership, which he also finds encouraging as he feels that the business will then belong to both of them.

Mary

Mary doesn't think she really needs to re-train to go and work in a shop somewhere. The only problem is that she has never used a computerised till, but she supposes she will be shown how to use this when she eventually finds a job. She does decide to enrol at an evening class, however, to take a GCSE in English Language, something she has wanted to do for years. She feels this can only help with job applications.

Richard

Richard feels he did enough retraining whilst still in prison. He took all the courses he possibly could and he does not think he could cope with going to college. As he already has some relevant NVQ qualifications, he decides to just keep looking around for a job involving some kind of computer inputting. If time proves this to be an impossibility, he supposes he will have to go back to lorry driving.

Andrew

Andrew doesn't know what he wants to do so he finds it hard to think of any specific training that will help him. He thinks his degree will be the passport to his success, even though he has never put it to good use before. At times he thinks of training for something really exciting but then decides it would be too much of an effort. He completely lacks any form of motivation. One day he visits his local Jobcentre and he is surprised at how helpful they are. He is given information about Career Development Loans and decides to give serious thought to training for accountancy. He has always enjoyed figures and thinks accountancy sounds a very respectable career to go for.

CHECKLIST

- Have you given enough thought to retraining?
- Are you prepared to try hard to succeed?
- Do you know what is available to you?
- Have you visited your local Jobcentre?
- Do you know what your local college could offer?
- Are you keeping yourself up to date by watching television and reading books?

POINTS FOR DISCUSSION

1   Write down what you see as the advantages and disadvantages of, firstly, attending a college of further education and, secondly, a privately run smaller college.

2   Make a list of the television programmes you usually watch. Do you think any of them help you to keep up with modern working trends? Make another list of the jobs portrayed in these programmes. Do any of them appeal to you?

3   Do you think there are enough government sponsored training schemes? Give the reasons for your answer.

4
Communicating with Others

USING POSITIVE BODY LANGUAGE

What is body language?

Body language, or non verbal communication as it is often called, is a way of communicating by using different parts of our body. A gesture, a nod of the head, a smile, might either accompany a conversation with someone, or be used alone. After all, a smile conveys a completely different meaning to a scowl, even if no words are spoken.

Most of the messages we convey by using body language are deliberate, but sometimes an involuntary message, such as a shiver, can escape without us even consciously thinking about it.

Body language is often said to be showing the emotional side of our relationships with people and positive body language is likely to produce a positive reaction from those around us.

It is important to use your body language to good effect. It can say far more than the words that accompany it. Other people can be very perceptive and if you look bored or raise your eyes to the ceiling in annoyance, the chances are it will be noticed. Whilst at home you will probably not have worried too much about your body language, but if you are returning to work, you may have to learn to hide your real feelings sometimes and at least pretend to be interested in what others say to you. We all meet boring people in our lives, but it is not always a good idea to show that you find them boring!

In the same way as you will have been taught to think before opening your mouth to speak, so you should try to control your body language and make it work for you in an effective and desirable manner, sending out the right rather than the wrong signals. Watch the signals from others too. In an interview, for example, by watching as well as listening to your interviewer, you will know whether or not you are making a good impression.

Examples of positive and negative body language

- **Eye contact**

  Positive: looking the other person in the eye as you speak

  Negative: looking away and showing disinterest

- **Sitting**

  Positive: sitting up straight, looking alert and confident

  Negative: slouching in the chair with your head down

- **Closeness**

  Positive: sitting or standing close to the person you are talking to

  Negative: keeping your distance and appearing wary

- **Habits**

  Positive: no annoying habits to irritate others

  Negative: drumming your fingers, biting your nails, scratching your head etc

- **Head movements**

  Positive: nodding and shaking your head to show agreement or disagreement

  Negative: not showing any head movements at all

- **Facial expressions**

  Positive: a smile or a frown according to the situation

  Negative: showing no expression in your face

Fig. 4. Examples of positive and negative body language.

LEARNING TO STICK UP FOR YOURSELF

If you have been out of the working world for some years, there is every chance that your self confidence will have taken a battering. Returning to work means, above all else, that you will have to learn to stick up for yourself once more. Whether you are returning to an employed or self employed job, sticking up for yourself will be an essential requirement.

The business world is tough and you will have to become tough too. Retiring into the corner like a quivering wreck every time someone upsets you will get you nowhere. Instead, if you retaliate — politely — you might not actually solve anything but you will at least feel better about the situation.

In order to help you stick up for yourself, try the following:

- Tell your partner/friend, anyone, what *you* want out of *your* life
- Tell your children/partner that this weekend *you* are going to choose where to go for the Sunday afternoon outing
- Go and complain next time you are charged wrongly at the super-market
- Write a letter to your local newspaper commenting on something that is upsetting you in your community
- Attend a local meeting and make sure you say something to contribute
- Give *your* views on politics/religion/world matters etc, next time a discussion takes place with friends, rather than just agreeing with what they say

JOINING A CLUB OR ORGANISATION

Joining a club or organisation is an excellent way of communicating with others. Obviously there are thousands of options available to you, such as:

- *A sports or social club*
  If you have a particular interest such as tennis, bowling, golf or dancing, then joining a club where like-minded people come together to share that interest can be a very enjoyable way of meeting people. Talk to them about their lives and their jobs and aim to find out as much as you can about current working trends. Get involved in organising special events. Go to any meetings they may hold and make sure you put your point of view at those meetings.

- *A drama club*
  If you tend to be the retiring sort, then joining a drama club is an excellent idea. Standing on a stage, speaking to an audience — if you can make yourself do it that first time — will do wonders for your self confidence. Even if you cannot bring yourself to act, there are plenty of other jobs to do, such as organising costumes, making the scenery and arranging publicity for forthcoming events.

- *Your local Parish Council*
  What better way is there of making sure you know all about changes in your local community than to join the Parish Council? You might think the meetings they hold are not much fun, but you would have the opportunity to get involved with what should concern you. You never know, you might add a positive sparkle to their previously dull existence.

- *School Parent/Teachers Association*
  If you have a child at school, you might well be invited to join the PTA. PTAs arrange events to raise funds for the school and generally assist in the non-academic side of school life.

DOING SOME VOLUNTARY WORK

If you are not returning to work just to earn money, then doing some voluntary work can be very rewarding, either on a temporary basis until you find paid employment, or as a permanent occupation. (See *How to Do Voluntary Work Abroad*, which also covers the UK voluntary sector, in this series.)

Just like clubs and organisations, so there are literally thousands of voluntary organisations.. Some seem more worthwhile than others, but presumably all of them exist to offer help to someone, somewhere. A very brief selection are:

- *The Citizens Advice Bureau*
  Most of you will know something of the principles behind the Citizens Advice Bureau. As their name suggests, they exist to offer advice to everyone, whether they are rich or poor, and whatever problems they may have. (They do not, however, deal directly with marital problems. These are dealt with by Relate.) There is close liaison between the Citizens Advice Bureau and professional people such as solicitors, accountants, councils etc, so if you work

for them you will gain a very good insight into what goes on in the world around you. They offer full training.

- *The Samaritans*
  The Samaritans deal with people's problems too, but more in the emotional sense. They offer help by telephone to those who are depressed, despairing, suicidal, scared, or unable to face up to their problems for any reason. You will be known by a first name only and your job will be to listen sympathetically to often desperate people. This is probably not a good job if you easily get upset yourself.

- *Hospital work*
  Hospital visiting, driving people to hospital, and general fund raising work offer a variety of ways to practise your communication skills, whilst at the same time carrying out a very useful job of work.

- *Helping with a local charity*
  Local charities always seem to need people to help out in their shops, with collections and fund raising events. If you can choose a charity close to your own heart, then so much the better. If you are considering shop work as paid employment, working in a charity shop can be a good way to start.

TALKING TO DIFFERENT PEOPLE

Whenever we talk to someone, either on the telephone or in person, we are communicating. Unfortunately, this does not necessarily mean that what we communicate is particularly interesting or useful.

If you have, for instance, been at home with children for many years, then your main conversation with friends has probably centred around potty training, little Billy's first day at school and what to get for dinner at night. When you return to work, the chances are that your workmates will not be terribly keen to hear about such things, so you need to get some serious conversation practice in first.

Start by reading the newspaper every day. Watch the evening news and some factual programmes on television. Try out your new-found topics of conversation with your partner first, then with your friends, and see what response you get. If you have friends who lead interesting lives and have interesting jobs, talk to them about what they do. Learn from other people and their experiences. Be aware of what goes on around you. You'll be surprised at just what you find out.

Once you have broadened your horizons, you will start to feel more confident about your ability to communicate effectively. You will be saying the things that people want to hear. Your conversations will command attention.

CASE STUDIES

Sue

Sue's main interest in life is her children. Because of this she decides to join the PTA at their school. In no time at all she is involved in organising the annual barbecue, writing to the parents, getting tickets printed and approaching local businesses for raffle prizes. To her surprise she finds she really enjoys herself and she begins to feel more confident about her ability to do something worthwhile in the working world too.

Paula

Paula has no time for anyone other than herself and would never consider any kind of voluntary work. She belongs to the local tennis club where she occasionally goes, but, apart from her special friend Lucy, she tries to speak to as few people as possible. She considers her own life is far too important to worry about others, even though she is intending to work in what is generally thought of as a 'caring role'.

John

John belongs to the local drama group. He is about to play the lead part in a production for the first time and is very nervous. At the last minute he feels sure he will never be able to do it, but he forces himself and finds out just how exhilarating acting on a stage can be. For the first time in years he feels he has done something for himself and something he can be proud of. He receives rave reviews in the local paper and from his partner too.

Mary

Mary's tutor at her English evening class watches her closely one evening, trying to decide exactly what sort of person she is. She sits very upright in her sea, but always with her head down, and she will never look him in the eye. When he asks her to answer a question she jumps nervously and then mumbles the correct answer, turning bright red as she does so. Her face shows very little expression and she never laughs.

The tutor comes to the conclusion that Mary is lacking in self confidence, although she does have the ability to succeed. She appears to him to be mildly depressed and seems to need something exciting to happen to shake her out of her insular little world.

Richard

Richard meets an old friend in the High Street one day. They went to school together, but Richard has not heard of or seen him since he came out of prison. The conversation goes thus:

'Hello Dave, long time no see. How are you?' Richard smiles at his old friend and holds out his hand.

'Hello Richard,' answers Dave, refusing the outstretched hand and edging away. 'I'm fine.'

'How about a drink one night, say tomorrow?' asks Richard.

'No, sorry mate, I don't mix with ex-cons,' answers Dave sneeringly.

'Listen, I've done my time, I've learnt my lesson and now I have a family to consider. I have no intention of ever getting into trouble again, and who are you to talk anyway? You were put on probation some years ago. Were you given a chance afterwards? Did I stop mixing with you then?' Richard is very annoyed at his so-called friend's attitude.

Dave begins to look a little sheepish.

'Okay, sorry mate. I suppose a drink wouldn't do any harm, as long as you're paying.' Dave laughs as though he has said something funny.

'No, don't bother, Dave. I'm fussy who I drink with anyway. Friends like you I can do without, thanks.' Without waiting for a reply Richard stalks off.

As you will see from this conversation, Richard has had to learn to be tough. He knows people will victimise him and he knows he deserves it, but he feels he should have his say too. He has learned the hard way that he will have to stick up for himself if he is to get anywhere in his life.

Andrew

Andrew decides to join The Samaritans, really to see if other people have the same problems as him. After a few weeks he becomes very depressed himself and it is suggested that he gives it up. The people he works with can see straight away that Andrew is a man with his own serious problems. They do not think he is a good influence on the people who call on him for help.

CHECKLIST

- Is your body language saying what you want it to say?

- Have you spent some time just watching other people?

- Can you stand up for yourself when you need to?

- Do you belong to a club or organisation where you can communicate with people outside your home environment?

- Have you thought about doing some voluntary work?

- Are you trying to further your knowledge of what goes on in the world?

- Can you talk to other people about anything other than your home life.

POINTS FOR DISCUSSION

1 How do you think positive body language will help you at a job interview?

2 What would you do if the neighbours suddenly stopped talking to you and you didn't know the reason why?

3 Preferably working with a partner, make a list of important world events over the last week. How many could you talk about confidently?

5
Regaining Confidence

LEARNING TO BELIEVE IN YOURSELF

In order to survive in the working world of today you must believe in your ability to succeed. After all, if you cannot convince yourself that you are worth believing in, then how can you hope to convince someone else?

Ask yourself a few questions:

- What have you succeeded at in the past?
- What hopes and ambitions have you for the future?
- What can you change in your life to make yourself feel more confident?
- Have you got the backing of a loving partner?
- Do you think you are capable of more than you are doing at the moment?

If you can answer these questions in a positive, rather than a negative way, then you are well on your way to believing in yourself once more. When that stage is reached you stand a pretty good chance of convincing someone else that you are worth taking seriously.

IDENTIFYING YOUR GOOD POINTS

It is best not to dwell for too long on your bad points. Instead, identify your good points and then think about how to put them to good use. Are you:

- Honest and trustworthy?
- Pleasant in appearance?
- Reasonably intelligent?
- Eager to learn?

- Considerate of other people?
- Hard working?

If you have answered 'yes' to at least four of these questions then you should certainly prove to be an asset at work, even if you do not have any recent job experience.

Now let us look at what you can actually do:

- Can you use a keyboard?
- Can you supervise other people?
- Do you have a particular skill to offer?
- Do you have any qualifications?
- Do you have any past experience?
- Do you have a basic knowledge of grammar, spelling and punctuation?
- Can you write coherently?
- Would you be able to cope in a crisis?

If you have answered 'yes' to at least six out of these eight questions, then once again, the world of work beckons.

OVERCOMING SHYNESS

If you are naturally shy, there is no point in saying to you that if you follow a set course of action your shyness will disappear, as if by magic, because it will not. It is possible, however, to examine the reasons why you are shy and to look at ways of slowly overcoming such feelings.

Shyness often dates back to childhood. Perhaps you had a parent, or a sister or brother, who continually undermined your efforts. Perhaps you were an only child who spent most of your time at home with friends or relatives. Perhaps you suffered the break up of a relationship which was very important to you.

It is equally possible that you did not feel shy at all until your break from work. The realisation that the business world has changed in your absence and that everyone around you seems so competent and self assured can lead to a shyness which is not really your natural self.

If you do feel shy, whatever the reason, try the following:

- Make yourself talk to as many people as possible. It doesn't matter who they are - friends, relatives, people in the supermarket.

- Look interested in what others have to say. You do not want to give the impression of being aloof and stand-offish when really you are only shy.

- Take a closer look at those around you, particularly people you admire. Are they as confident as they at first appear? Underneath their tough exterior they probably feel just as insecure as you, but maybe they have learned to cover it up.

- Next time you see someone on television who seems perfectly poised and in command of life, imagine them having their morning bath in cold water because the hot has run out, pushing the car up the drive because they left the lights on, and swearing as they spill coffee on their smart new suit. You see, they too are just as human as you are, with just as many of life's little problems to contend with.

Although shyness is a very real problem, it can be overcome if you make a real effort. What you have to remember is that there really is no need to feel shy with anyone, no matter how important they are. Your contribution to the outside world is just as important as theirs, maybe more so. Just think what everyone has been missing during your years away from work!

MAKING MATURITY AN ASSET

You should never think of your maturity as a handicap. It can, and should, be used to your advantage.

Whether you are thinking of self employment or employed work, maturity is likely to help rather than hinder your efforts. Yes, of course there will always be job advertisements that ask for 'school leavers', 'someone under 25' etc, but there will, if you look, be far more jobs saying 'mature person preferred'. With self employment too, experience of life will help you to cope with the hassles and complications of setting up in business, along with the likely disappointments along the way.

Please try not to listen to spoilsports (particularly your offspring), who may say things like 'where are you going to get a job at *your* age?' If you have the right qualifications, the right attitude and the right approach, you will find out that your maturity can work for, rather than against, your chances of employment.

Employers are not silly. They know that, for instance, a woman of 45 is likely to stay with them for perhaps 15 years. How many young girls of 21 would do the same? Reliability usually comes with maturity too. An older person who has worked to a set routine for a number of years knows that order and a responsible approach are important requirements for everyday life, either at home or in the workplace.

A special note here for mothers or indeed househusband fathers. It is often said that if you have coped for a number of years with bringing up young children, cleaning the house, doing the shopping, washing, ironing and catering for your other half's every whim, you have gained that particular kind of experience that cannot be learned at college, or from books. It is called the experience of sheer survival and it proves that you are a very special kind of person, who should be well able to cope with any crisis you ever meet in your working life!

SORTING OUT YOUR WARDROBE AND MAKE UP

This applies rather more to women than men, particularly the make up part! Men do, of course, need to look smart and may have to take stock of their wardrobe when returning to work. Flared trousers are no longer 'in' and scruffy jeans will not go down well either. Not as many organisations insist on male employees wearing suits as used to be the case, but it is always best to check on what is considered appropriate before you start a new job.

Women seem to have far more fashion worries than men. At home, casual clothes are usually the norm, but in the workplace, tastes and ideas can vary enormously. Unfortunately, in some organisations, standards have dropped and almost anything goes, but the vast majority of the working population is still expected to conform with tradition and wear smart clothes for work. Banks, building societies, shops, etc, provide uniforms for their staff. This saves any worries over what to wear. For everyone else, however, choosing clothes for work can cause a major headache.

If you can afford it, splash out on some new **clothes** to go with your new working image. There is no need to choose clothes that you know you will feel uncomfortable in. Instead, choose items that are smart, but at the same time make you feel good about yourself. If you are really out of touch with what is being worn, flick through a few magazines (not necessarily fashion magazines), for ideas.

Carefully applied **makeup** will make you look and feel good too. The emphasis should be on makeup that looks natural. Nothing looks worse than a mature lady walking around with inches of face paint and running mascara. On the other hand, subtle makeup will make you look and feel younger.

Perfume is another area where caution needs to be exercised. Strong pongs of violet or musk are guaranteed to send your workmates scurrying to the other end of the room. Something more refined, however, should prove very acceptable. Whilst on the subject of 'pongs', do make sure that you use an effective deodorant. This of course, applies equally to men and women. Word will get round very quickly if a member of staff has a 'personal hygiene' problem!

Finally, treat yourself to a good, easily managed, **haircut**. Nothing too fancy, but perhaps a change from your usual look. After all, the more you boost your confidence by paying attention to your appearance, the more chance you will find of firstly getting a job, and secondly keeping it!

CASE STUDIES

Sue

Sue knows that if she is going to take on some temporary work she will need to have some smart clothes to wear. As she never seems to have any money to buy clothes for herself, she decides to choose a few items from her friend's mail order catalogue. Her wardrobe at the moment consists of jeans, shirts and baggy jumpers, which are fine for home, but not too good for her new working image.

At one of the PTA meetings Sue gets talking to a hairdresser called Robert. She has not had her hair cut for years and longs for an up-to-date modern style. Sue plucks up the courage to ask Robert if he will cut and style it for her. She is thrilled with the result and now feels ready to face the world.

Paula

Paula has no problem believing in herself, or identifying her good points, and she is certainly not shy. As far as wardrobe and appearance are concerned, she spends a great deal of her husband's money on both, and considers herself to be immaculately dressed and groomed.

John

Following his drama success, John begins to believe in himself and his ability to succeed in whatever he sets his mind to. This spurs him on with his research into setting up in business. He attends the courses arranged for him under the Business Start Up Scheme and is told that he will qualify for the weekly allowance payable over the first 40 weeks.

Like many men, John does not have much clothes sense. His partner buys most of his clothes and he quite likes it that way. He is no follower of fashion but he does like to look smart.

Mary

Mary feels so depressed one morning that she takes herself out and has her hair done. Much to her surprise her husband says how nice it looks. That spurs her on to have a close look at her wardrobe. She has neglected herself for years and she sees now that all her clothes are dreadfully old fashioned and dull.

As she is so unsure of what to buy, Mary asks her married daughter, Amy, to go out shopping with her. Together they choose several smart outfits. Mary's mother left her some money so she can afford to be extravagant for once, and she treats her daughter too.

Mary's husband shows his approval again which makes her begin to feel better about her life in general. For the first time she begins to feel more confident.

Richard

Richard was encouraged to think about his good points whilst in prison. At first he didn't think he had any, but as time went on he began to realise that he was capable of proving himself if he put his mind to it.

Shyness is not a problem for him. He does lack confidence, but always shows a brash, slightly cocky approach to other people, and he finds it very easy to mix. His lack of confidence stems from his unhappy childhood when he was made to feel inadequate by his domineering father. He felt then as he does now, that he has to hide his true feelings from other people.

Andrew

Andrew is not shy either. He is a likeable person, although many of his friends feel that he needs to grow up. Like Richard his lack of confidence is well hidden, but unlike Richard he has a degree and a very good brain, both of which are going to waste.

Andrew is a very showy dresser. He tends to wear outrageous clothes and his girlfriend tells him that he will need to choose some more conservative outfits for any forthcoming job interviews.

CHECKLIST

- Have you given some serious thought to your future?

- Do you know your good points?

- Are you willing to work hard?

- If you are shy, what do you intend to do about it?

- Are you portraying your maturity as an asset?

- Does your wardrobe need a 'revamp'?

- Could you do with some personal tidying up?

- Are you mentally and physically prepared for the world of work?

POINTS FOR DISCUSSION

1   Do you think that what you wear to work is important? What clothes would you choose for the first day in a new job?

2   How would you approach a work colleague who suffers from BO, or wouldn't you?

3   Write down the reasons why you think an employer should choose you, a returner to work, rather than a college leaver for the vacancy he is advertising.

6
Coping with Technology

LOOKING ALL AROUND YOU

We live in a technological age. As each year goes by it seems that yet another sophisticated device is invented. Although these devices are designed to aid rather than complicate the lives of the prospective users, they can be a little daunting at first, to say the least.

Without thinking about the business world, you only need to look around your own house to see how things have changed over the last ten or 20 years. Many of you will use a microwave oven, an electronic washing machine and a dishwasher. Your television may be fitted with Ceefax and Oracle, you probably use a video recorder and may have a satellite dish too. Your boiler could well be electronically programmed. Your telephone may remember the last call you dialled and store commonly used numbers for you. The list is endless and if you really take the time to investigate you will probably be amazed at just how 'hi-tech' your home has become!

Outside the home, supermarkets have electronic scanning equipment, so not only do you receive an itemised bill, but the products are automatically re-ordered at the same time. Banks and building societies work almost exclusively from their computer terminals. Factories contain sophisticated machinery. Even the man on the market stall walks around with his mobile phone and pocket calculator.

Every office contains at least one computer system, a fax machine (see page 55) and lots of other electronic gadgetry, all designed to make life easier and output more cost effective.

When you return to work you will be caught up in this 'New Age' whether you like it or not, and the better prepared you are the easier you will cope.

LEARNING KEYBOARD SKILLS

'Keyboard skills' is a term used to describe what used to be called 'typing'. Now that the majority of people use computer keyboards rather than typewriters, typing is often called 'keyboarding' or 'keying in'.

It really is a good idea to learn keyboard skills whatever job you are planning to take on. Almost everyone has to use a keyboard at some time in their job nowadays. Even the good old family doctor is confronted with a VDU (Visual Display Unit) and keyboard every time he wants to issue a prescription. If you look carefully next time you go to see your own doctor you will probably see that he or she does not do it properly either. One finger keyboarding seems to be the norm.

Many people think it is too much effort to learn to use a keyboard properly but about ten hours concentrated work should be sufficient for the vast majority to be able to use the correct fingers without looking at the keyboard, which is what the old fashioned term 'touch typing' is all about.

TERMS USED IN THE ELECTRONIC OFFICE

CPU (Central Processing Unit)
This is the 'brain' of a computer.

Data
Information which can appear as words, numbers or symbols.

Database
Recorded data which can be retrieved and updated.

Disk/Diskette
Storage medium used by many computers. The disk is known as either a floppy disk, which means it is inserted into the machine, or a hard disk which forms part of the computer's CPU.

Disk drive
The slot in a computer into which the disk is inserted.

File
A single computer document. Each file may contain just one document or several. Files can be kept together in electronic directories.

Graphics
Illustrations, such as charts, graphs etc, that are drawn by means of a computer.

Hard copy
Printout (on paper).

Hardware
The mechanical, electronic and outer casing of a computer, *ie*, CPU, VDU and keyboard.

IT (information technology)
A general term used to cover all the technology used to input, store, retrieve, change, and send out information.

Mail merge
A 'mail merge' is when information from two computer files is combined. This then enables, for instance, the names and addresses of a list of people to be merged with a standard letter.

Network
A string of computer devices that are linked together.

Software
The programs run on computer hardware.

Spreadsheet
An electronic worksheet containing data in various columns and rows which can perform automatic calculations. Used for accounts work.

VDU (Visual Display Unit)
A screen linked to a computer system.

GETTING TO GRIPS WITH WORD PROCESSING

Word processing is, as its name suggests, the processing of words. This is normally carried out on a computer using a word processing package, of which there are many. It must be remembered, of course, that computers are also capable of many other functions as well as word processing, depending on the program being used at the time.

While text is being keyed in it can be changed as required. When the document is finished it can be printed out and/or stored to be used at a future date. At any time the text can be changed or updated by calling back the document onto your screen.

Using a computer with a word processing package is a far easier way of producing documents than the conventional typewriter. You will see why when you look at what most word processing programs can do (see Fig. 5).

In theory, by using a word processing package, it should be possible to produce a perfect document every time. Unfortunately, however, the machine will only do what the operator tells it to, so it is possible for human error to creep in every now and again!

Printing the documents

There are three main types of printer available at present:

Dot matrix

This operates by forming dots using a series of needles. Generally speaking the more needles the better the result. Hence a 9 pin printer will not perform as well as a 24 pin printer. Early dot matrix printers gave poor results, but they have improved a good deal over the years and a good dot matrix printer should give perfectly adequate, if not outstanding, quality suitable for most business uses.

Ink jet

Ink jet printers throw minute jets of ink rapidly on to the paper. They give a much more professional look to documents than dot matrix printers. Running costs used to be high but they have come down quite considerably recently.

Ink jet printers are ideal for the small business user who wants to produce good quality copy at a reasonable price and speed.

Laser

This comes top of the popular printer range. The machine is similar in appearance and operation to a photocopier. It is faster than either the dot matrix or the ink jet and can handle vast quantities of paper in no time at all, producing top class copies. The down side is that it is the most expensive of the three to buy and can be expensive to run too. Costs are coming down, however, and many organisations find that the advantages outweigh the extra capital outlay and running costs.

USING THE POST OR SENDING A FAX?

Another electronic marvel is the facsimile machine or 'Fax' as it is more commonly known. A fax sends a copy of your document through

Some functions of word-processing

- Show text on a screen

- Store text

- Add, delete or re-arrange text

- Copy text from one document to another

- Correct text before printing

- Justify text so that the left and right margins are equal

- Adjust margins so that parts of the text stand out from the rest

- Centre text, which is useful for headings

- Underline text and highlight headings etc in bold type

- Spellcheck the text

- Search for specific words or phrases in the text

- Add 'headers' and 'footers' to text (*ie*, page numbers, titles etc)

- Display text in columns

- Change line spacing, pitch size and print style (in conjunction with the printer being used)

- Merge names and addresses with standard letters

Fig. 5. Some functions of word-processing.

the telephone network to another machine anywhere in the world. It is particularly useful for diagrams, legal documents and all urgent correspondence.

It works as follows:

1. Two fax machines are linked by means of telephone lines

2. You place the original document in the tray of your fax machine

3. The recipient's fax number is dialled

4. The recipient's machine reproduces a facsimile of the original.

Even a small business can afford a fax machine. The big plus point of sending a fax of a document rather than using the postal system is the speed of transmission. The document arrives instantly, whereas with the normal post it would not arrive until the next day at the very earliest. There is a minus point too, however, in that the quality of the reproduction is not as good as the original.

The best plan is to fax very urgent documents and send the rest by post in the traditional way.

CASE STUDIES

Sue

Sue is really keen to understand as much as possible about every aspect of new technology. She finds it all very exciting and enjoyed her word processing course very much. Her friend has her own computer and tells Sue that she can use it whenever she likes. This computer came with a pre-loaded package which includes spreadsheets, graphics and a basic word processing program, so Sue has plenty to experiment with.

Although she has not yet been given any assignments by the agency, Sue feels she is adding to her skills all the time by using her friend's computer and she is considering paying for another course at the private college she attended to take a higher qualification.

Another friend runs a small secretarial services bureau, and she asks Sue if she would like to help out there on a couple of mornings each week, just to gain some up to date office experience. She learns to use a fax and a colour photocopier, as well as Wordstar, another popular word processing program.

Paula

Paula knows very little about any new office technology. She has every possible electronic gadget in the house and is familiar with a fax machine but that is about all. Her husband has a computer but Paula never uses it. She thinks she is above mundane office work anyway. When she opens her nursing home she will have staff to do that sort of thing for her. She steadfastly refuses to get involved in anything other than her search for suitable premises.

John

John gets a book out of the library and teaches himself keyboarding skills. They have a computer at home so he is able to practise and he soon becomes quite proficient. He knows that when he starts his little business he will not have enough money to employ someone to do his correspondence, so he is determined to learn the necessary skills. He starts to produce some course notes to work from when he begins teaching his students. He finds that typewritten notes are far easier to read than his usual scrawl!

Mary

Mary is still looking for a part-time shop job. Computers do not interest her at all. Her big worry is that she has never used a computerised till. She finally plucks up the courage to ask a shop owner friend if she could possibly show her how such a till works. The friend is only too pleased to help and Mary ends up working in the shop for a few hours each week just to get back into the swing of things. Mary refuses payment, saying that the experience is what she wants and her friend is very grateful for the extra help.

Richard

Richard, rather like Sue, loves anything to do with new technology. He has become very proficient in using a computer with a variety of different programs, and whilst he was in prison he learnt to use the keyboard properly too. He seems to have a natural ability, and spends hours using the computer they bought secondhand from a local dealer. All he longs for now is a job using a computer so that he can begin to earn some honest money from what he enjoys doing.

Andrew

Andrew is very proficient with his mobile phone. He uses it on every possible occasion. He has also purchased a fax, more for his image than anything else, because he really doesn't have any faxes to send. He can use a computer but is not really very keen, although he knows that if he takes up accountancy he will be using a screen for a good deal of the time. He finds sitting in one place for any length of time very boring and he gets fidgety, so he is having second thoughts about his accountancy idea anyway.

CHECKLIST

- How much has technology changed your life at home?
- Have you mastered all your home 'gadgets'?
- Can you use a keyboard properly?
- Do you understand the terms used in the electronic office?
- Can you use a word processing package?
- Do you understand what word processing is all about?
- Are you familiar with the different printers available?
- Do you know how to send a fax?
- Do you know when to send a fax?
- Have you acquired sufficient knowledge to cope with the technology of today?

POINTS FOR DISCUSSION

1   How important do you think it is for everyone to learn keyboard skills? Do you think this should be taught in schools along with computer studies?

2   Do you think computers help or hinder our everyday life? Give reasons for your answer.

3   Do you prefer the modern supermarket with sophisticated scanning equipment, or the older style store where the assistant stops for a chat while she rings up each item individually on the till? With which system do you think the most mistakes are made?

7
Applying for Jobs

KNOWING WHERE TO LOOK

Having got to the stage of actually applying for jobs there are three chief places to look for vacancies.

Your local Jobcentre
Vacancies are advertised on cards either in the window or in racks inside, and you can ask about anything that interests you. The staff in Jobcentres are usually very helpful and if you cannot find anything suitable on the cards, you can always ask them about your chances of finding what you are looking for. They are there to help you and should be able to offer some good advice.

Newspaper advertisements
Most of the national and regional newspapers have set days for job advertisements; some concentrate on different types of jobs — *eg*, teaching — on different days of the week. Make sure you scan the papers well and cut out any advertisements offering jobs that appeal to you. Read the advertisement carefully to check how your application is to be made — by 'phone, by letter, by application form, or by CV.

Private Employment Agencies
Agencies are particularly useful for temp work. If this is what you are looking for, it is a good idea to register with a couple of agencies, to see who finds work for you first. Most agencies also have clients on their books who are looking for permanent staff. As agencies charge the employers a hefty amount for finding permanent staff, however, many organisations find it far cheaper to place an advertisement in the Jobcentre or local newspaper.

Apart from these sources, it is also possible to find jobs in other ways. You may be talking to someone who happens to mention that Bloggs and Son are looking for a clerical assistant. You may see an advertisement in a shop window asking for a sales assistant. Supermarkets and other large stores often advertise their vacancies on a board by the main entrance.

If you really want to show initiative, you could send a few tentative letters to employers who just might have the sort of position you are looking for. You never know. Your letter could arrive on someone's desk on exactly the same day as a letter of resignation from one of their employees!

KNOWING WHAT TO LOOK FOR

It is very important that when you look for a job you try to match your skills and experience to the job being offered. There is no shortage of applicants for most vacancies, so those with the most suitable backgrounds are likely to be the ones selected for interview.

For instance, a job vacancy for a medical secretary is more likely to be filled by someone with a knowledge of medical terminology than by a person who worked as a legal secretary before taking her career break. In the same way, a person recently released from prison after serving a sentence for burglary is unlikely to be given a job as a double glazing salesman, thus gaining access into homes and being allowed the opportunity to weigh up the prospects.

When you see a vacancy that interests you, ask yourself these questions:

- Am I qualified to do this job?
- Do I have the relevant experience?
- Can I manage the hours?
- Is the salary what I need?
- Will I be able to travel easily to and from work?

If you can answer 'yes' to these questions then the job sounds worth applying for.

SENDING A LETTER OF APPLICATION

Most advertisements will ask you to write if you are interested in a vacancy. This letter of application is very important as it is the first contact you are making with your prospective employer.

Nowadays when a job is advertised in a newspaper, quite possibly hundreds, or in some cases even thousands, of people will apply. You have got to make your application stand out against the rest.

Valley Rise
Raleigh Road
HADFLEET
Sussex
BN12 9LT

14 March 199X

Mr T Barrett
Medical Records Officer
Royal Infirmary
Tanner Road
BLYFORD
Sussex
BN17 0RD

Dear Mr Barrett

I would like to apply for the part-time position of Medical Secretary in the Gynaecology Department, as advertised in Friday's edition of the Evening Echo.

Although I have not worked in an employed capacity for the past twelve years, I have been kept busy working for Healthwatch, as you will see from the enclosed Curriculum Vitae. Now my children are in full-time education, however, I would very much like to return to work. My mother lives with us and she is available to look after the children during the school holidays.

If you consider my application to be of interest, I shall be pleased to attend for interview.

Yours sincerely

Sarah Louise Barker   (Mrs)

enc: CV

Fig. 6. A sample letter of application.

It is usual to send a Curriculum Vitae (CV) with your letter of application. (See the next section for how to compile a CV.) For this reason the letter can be short, because most of the relevant information will be contained in the accompanying CV. The letter can be typed or handwritten, unless the advertisement specifically mentions one or the other.

The letter of application should say what you are applying for and where you saw the advertisement. It needs to contain brief details of why you think you would be suitable for the job, and the closing paragraph should mention that you would be pleased to attend for interview. See the example on p 62.

PREPARING A RETURNER'S CV

CV or Curriculum Vitae actually means 'the course of your life' and it should give a prospective employer all the information he or she needs to judge whether you will make a suitable candidate for interview. Your personal details, your schooling, your qualifications and your work record, need to be displayed in a clear, easy to read, way. Explain any gaps in your working record. Your CV should be typed, so if you do not have keyboard skills yourself, ask a friend or an agency to prepare it for you. It must look professional and be error-free. An example of a returner's CV is given on page 64, to give you a framework from which to compile your own.

BEING PATIENT

Looking for a job is rather like trying to sell your house. You just have to be patient. One day, hopefully sooner rather than later, you will apply for a job, get an interview and be offered the position, but in between be prepared for many disappointments.

The job market is competitive and employers can be as choosy as they wish. The only real way you can help yourself is by making sure you apply for suitable jobs where you should stand some chance, sell yourself in your letter of application and CV and then leave the rest to luck and good fortune.

Please try not to get too despondent. The right job will come along eventually and then all your efforts will have been worthwhile. In the meantime try to exercise a degree of patience and carry on enjoying life while you wait for success.

C U R R I C U L U M   V I T A E

Name:	Sarah Louise BARKER		
Address:	Valley Rise		
	Raleigh Road		
	HADFLEET		
	Sussex		
	BN12 9LT		
Telephone number:	01254-713450		
Date of birth:	24 June 1954		
Marital status:	Married		
Nationality:	British		
Education:	The Royal School for Girls		1965-1972
	Lapworth College		1972-1974
Qualifications:	GCE 'O' Levels:		
	English Language	Grade A	1970
	English Literature	Grade A	1970
	Mathematics	Grade C	1970
	History	Grade C	1970
	Geography	Grade C	1970
	GCE 'A' Levels:		
	English	Grade A	1972
	Association of Medical		
	Secretaries Diploma		1974
	RSA Stage III Typewriting		1974
	RSA 120 wpm Shorthand		1974
	RSA Stage III Sec Duties		1974
	RSA Stage III Word Proc		1994
Present employer:	Not working at present.		
	Last twelve years spent at home bringing up family.		
Previous experience:	Medical Secretary, St Ann's Hospital, Widmouth		1974-1982
Other relevant information:	Although I have not been officially working, I am Secretary for the local 'Healthwatch' Branch. This involves taking minutes and replying to correspondence. I have recently taken a refresher course and learned to use a PC with WordPerfect 5.1 as the program. I have a full driving licence.		
Interests:	Reading, tennis, squash		
Referees:	Available on request		

Fig. 7. A sample CV.

CASE STUDIES

For the next three chapters we will be looking at the fortunes of just four of our case studies. We will come back to Paula and John in Chapter 10 as they are both intending to become self employed rather than work for someone else.

Sue

Sue reads the following advertisement in the local paper:

> Clerical Assistant required. 15 hrs each week, term time only. Small, caring independent school. Knowledge of WordPerfect an advantage. Tel: The Secretary, Knolls Hill School, 01932-967845.

Although Sue has intended to work as a temp, this opportunity seems too good to miss so she telephones straight away. The Secretary sounds very friendly and invites Sue to send in her CV. This she does and receives a letter in reply asking her to attend for interview the following week.

Mary

After many months of searching Mary has seen a job advertised in the local supermarket for a part-time assistant. She asks for an application form and is told to send it back completed with a covering letter. Mary fills in the form and writes out her letter. She asks her friend at the shop to look at the letter. It reads like this:

34 High Street
Rumley
BROOME
Kent

Dear Sir

I spoke to you about the vacancy the other day and you said to fill in the form and send it back. I am doing this now. I hope you will find me suitable and I look forward to hearing from you.

Yours sincerely

Mary Jones

Mary's friend points out that, without wishing to be unkind, she thinks the letter could be better displayed and be worded slightly differently. The amended version looks like this:

34 High Street
Rumley
BROOME
Kent
TN12 8RT

16 May 199X

Mr J Smith
Branch Manager
Lowprices Superstore
BROOME
Kent
TN14 9HY

Dear Mr Smith

Part-time vacancy as General Assistant

With reference to our conversation the other day about the above
vacancy, I now have pleasure in returning the completed
application form, as requested.

I would be pleased to attend for an interview and I look forward to
hearing from you.

Yours sincerely

Mary Jones

enc

This letter looks and reads better. A date and postcode have been
inserted and the letter addresses the manager by name. It is likely to
attract a far more positive response.

Richard

Richard has decided to ask for professional advice about a CV and
covering letter. He wants to be honest, but on the other hand he does not
want to discourage prospective employers. This is the result:

CURRICULUM VITAE

Name: Richard O'Brien

Address: 4 Shiers Walk
BOLTON
Sussex
BN18 5TH

Telephone number: 01923-657231

Date of birth: 12 September 1966

Marital status: Single

Nationality: British

Education: Briar Comprehensive School 1977-1982

Qualifications:

GCE 'O' Levels:

English Language	Grade C	1982
History	Grade D	1982

CSE:

Mathematics	Grade 2	1982
Geography	Grade 3	1982
French	Grade 3	1982

NVQ Business Administration
Level II 1994

Present employer: Not working at present.
Recently released from Bloomsdale Prison.

Previous experience: Lorry Driver for: 1982-1989
R C Green & Co
Bolton

Other relevant information: During my time in prison I took several different courses, including several working with computers. As you will see I gained an NVQ in Business Administration.

Interests: Computers, reading, walking

Referees: On request

Outline letter to accompany CV

4 Shiers Walk
BOLTON
Sussex
BN18 5TH

Date

Name and address of person
advertising the vacancy

Dear

Re: Vacancy for _____

I would like to apply for the position of _____ advertised in _____.

I am 28 years of age and worked for seven years as a lorry driver for R C Green & Co. I have, I am ashamed to admit, just spent some time in Bloomsdale Prison, but I am now determined to lead a respectable life and make up for lost time.

As you will see from my CV, which is enclosed, whilst in Prison I gained the NVQ Business Administration, Level II qualification and I took several computer courses. My aim is to find a position where I can use computers and for this reason the vacancy you are offering is of particular interest.

I do hope you will give due consideration to my application. If you would like me to attend for an interview I shall be pleased to do so.

Yours sincerely

Richard O'Brien

enc

The CV together with a letter such as this should serve to show employers that Richard is serious about making a new start.

Andrew

Andrew has a problem. His CV looks most impressive until he reaches the 'Previous Experience' section. He has had so many jobs, most of them temporary, and he knows this will not look encouraging to a prospective employer. He asks for advice at his local Jobcentre and he is advised to try to group some of the jobs together. This is how it looks first of all:

Previous experience		
	Travel courier for Sun Holidays	1993-1994
	Travel courier for Roma Travel	1992-1993
	Travel rep for Malta Holidays	1991-1992
	Travel rep for Popular Tours	1990-1991
	Self employed as car hire owner in Italy	1987-1990
	Bar work in Hotel in America	1985-1987
	Worked in bar at Hotel in Italy	1982-1985
	Worked in bar at Hotel in France	1980-1982
	Sales Rep for Pussy Food Ltd	1978-1980
	Branch Manager, Plus Bdg Society	1975-1978
	Management Trainee, Plus Bdg Soc	1973-1975

The amended version is this:

Previous experience		
	Travel courier in various foreign resorts	1990-1994
	Care hire company in Italy — self employed	1987-1990
	Bar work in America, Italy and France	1980-1987
	Sales Rep for Pussy Foods Ltd	1978-1980
	Branch Manager, Plus Bdg Society	1975-1978
	Management Trainee, Plus Bdg Soc	1973-1975

The amended version still shows quite a few jobs but is easier to read and more likely to be treated seriously than the first version.

CHECKLIST

- Are you actively looking for jobs?
- Are you looking in the right places?

- Are your job applications realistic?
- Have you prepared a CV and a standard letter of application?
- Have you obtained photocopies of your CV so that they are ready to send out as necessary?
- Have you accepted that it might take time to find a job?
- Are you being patient?
- Are you getting on with your life in the meantime?

POINTS FOR DISCUSSION

1   Write out your own CV from the example given. Check it carefully and then either print out several copies or have the top copy photo-copied, ready for use when you apply for jobs.

2   List what you think would be the necessary qualities and skills for the following jobs:
Clerical assistant in council offices
Helping out in an old people's home
Taxi driver
Gardener

3   Do you think a CV gives more information than a company's own application form? Give the reasons for your answer.

8
Succeeding at an Interview

ACCEPTING THE INVITATION

Always take any opportunity offered to you to attend an interview. Even if you do not think the job offered is the one of your dreams, the experience is never wasted.

When you receive the telephone call or letter offering you an interview, first of all make sure you are able to attend. If you are genuinely unable to manage the date and time offered to you, ask for an alternative. Most organisations are fairly understanding and will re-schedule once. They may well become impatient, however, if you try to change an interview date more than once.

As soon as you have an interview arranged, find out as much as you can about the organisation in question. This will show that you have taken the trouble to research them and their activities and it will definitely go in your favour. If you have no idea what they do, who their parent company is, how many people are employed there etc, you will be hard pushed to carry on much of a conversation. Sounding as though you know what you are talking about will help the interview run smoothly.

TURNING UP ON TIME

If you are not sure how long it will take you to reach your interview destination, do a trial run first. Find out where to park your car or the times of public transport. Your aim should be to arrive about five minutes early, composed and looking relaxed (even if you do not feel it), rather than five minutes late and out of breath.

Remember that if you turn up late for an interview, however valid your reason, you will make your interviewer think that you are unreliable. That will not set the scene for a successful interview to follow.

71

GIVING A GOOD IMPRESSION

Apart from turning up on time, other ways of giving a good impression include wearing the right clothes and acting in the right way.

There is no need to rush out and spend hundreds of pounds on new clothes. Similarly, your scruffy jeans will not be suitable for most interview occasions either. The secret is to wear smart but comfortable clothes. Make sure that they are clean and well pressed. Above all, wear clothes that suit your personality. If you do, you will feel more at ease and it will show.

Acting in the right way can be a little more difficult to accomplish. Being interviewed for a job can be a nerve-wracking experience, particularly if it is a job you really need and want. If you are naturally shy and lacking in confidence, then work at doing something about it in advance. (See Chapter 5).

Tips

Here are a few tips that might help you to look and feel more at ease when attending an interview:

- Take several slow, deep breaths before entering the interview room.

- Smile at your interviewer as you enter the room and be ready to shake their hand.

- Sit down when asked to and do not start fiddling with anything. Sit straight in the chair and face your interviewer positively.

- Study your interviewer and try to read their body language. Perhaps he or she is showing signs of nerves too. You see, everyone is human!

- Remember to smile and say thank you to your interviewer when you leave. Last impressions can be as important as first impressions.

In an interview situation, the body language you use — *ie*, the way you react to your interviewer — will give either a bad or good impression of you as a person. If you frown when asked a question, look down at the floor as you answer, and raise your eyes to the ceiling when asked to take a simple test, you will be labelled as having an 'attitude' problem, even if your actual spoken words sound positive. If, on the other hand, you appear interested, look your interviewer in the eye, smile at the right time, and generally give the impression of wanting to be there, you will create a good impression.

Perhaps the most important point of all is that you must believe in yourself and your ability to do the job. If you are unsure of your suitability, then you cannot expect to convince your prospective employer and perhaps you should not be attending the interview in the first place.

BEING POSITIVE

The main part of any interview involves the interviewer asking you questions and you giving your answers. You will probably also be given some time at the end of the interview to ask some questions of your own.

Think very carefully about the questions you are likely to be asked and how you will answer them. For instance, if questions like 'Why do you think you are suitable for this position, Mr Jones?' or 'How will you manage the children during the school holidays?' are answered with 'Well, I haven't given it much thought really', you will not impress your interviewer very much! Advance preparation will mean that you should not get caught out with an awkward question that you cannot answer.

Once you have some interview experience you will notice a common theme of questions running through each and every interview you attend. After all, the aim of all interviewers is to find out as much as possible about you and your suitability for the job.

Types of question
There are two main types of questions that your interviewer will use:

Open questions
An example of an open question is: 'Tell me something about yourself'. This type of question requires a detailed answer. It does not, however, mean that you should waffle on and on until your interviewer becomes bored.

Closed questions
An example of a closed question is: 'What year did you start at Jones & Son?'. This type of question requires a direct and short answer.

Did I arrive on time?	Yes/No
Did I allow enough time to freshen up?	Yes/No
Did I dress appropriately?	Yes/No
Did I try to relax before being called in?	Yes/No
Did I shake hands confidently?	Yes/No
Did I remember the interviewer's name?	Yes/No
Did I maintain good eye contact?	Yes/No
Did I listen carefully to the questions?	Yes/No
Did I think before answering?	Yes/No
Did I speak clearly?	Yes/No
Did I smile at the right times?	Yes/No
Did I show that I had done my homework on the organisation?	Yes/No
Did I ask intelligent and sensible questions?	Yes/No
Did I thank the interviewer before leaving?	Yes/No
Did I make a positive impression?	Yes/No

If you answered No to any of these questions, try to correct it for the next interview.

Fig. 8. Reviewing that interview.

An effective interviewer will use the different types of questions for different reasons. The open questions tell the interviewer a lot about you as a person. The closed questions extract the facts.

As mentioned before, you will usually be given the opportunity at the end of an interview to ask some questions yourself. **Prepare a few in advance**, if only to show that you have given the matter some thought. Ask your questions politely, one at a time, and wait for the answer to one before moving on to the next.

STRESSING YOUR EXPERIENCE OF LIFE

Remember — your maturity is an asset, not a handicap. Keep saying that to yourself. You may not be 21 any more, but what you do have is experience of life. No-one can argue with that and you must play it up to the full.

When returning to work after a break it is very important that you say what you have been doing during your absence. If you have been at home with children, perhaps you have also run the Brownies, or belonged to the local Operatic Society. Have you been involved with community work, or helped out at the school? All these points are important to mention. They show you have done **something** with your time, apart from looking after the kids. Incidentally, if you do have children, make sure you spell out the cover you have arranged for them if they are ill or off school for any reason.

Similarly, a prison spell need not have been wasted. Emphasise the training courses and the work you did while inside. Spell out your plans for the future. Aim to convince the interviewer that you are making a fresh start.

Whatever the reason for your break, you have to try to convince your interviewer that now you are back and you intend to make a place for yourself at work once more. Stress your **loyalty**; how you will be able to stay with them for years, now that you are older and more stable; how you are a far better bet than a 21 year old female who is likely to leave her job at some time to start a family.

Remember to impress upon your interviewer the following:

- your **commitment** to a new start
- your **loyalty** to the organisation
- your **willingness** to adapt to new trends
- your **suitability** for the job on offer.

In general, interviews rarely turn out to be as frightening as you might be expecting. As long as you keep calm and tell yourself that you are just as good as anyone else, you should do just fine — even if you are not actually offered the job!

Attending one interview gives useful experience for the next and you should not be surprised or disappointed if you have to attend several interviews before being successful. After all, if 30 people are being interviewed for one position, 29 are going to be unlucky, even though they may all be potentially suitable candidates. Getting an interview at all, when there are often hundreds of applicants for a job, is a step in the right direction. One day though, luck will be on your side, and the interview will prove to be *the one*.

CASE STUDIES

Let us suppose that Sue, Mary, Richard and Andrew have someone to advise them on how to answer one of the standard interview questions. This means they can have a trial run before the big day. The question is:

'Tell me something about yourself and why you want to work for us.'

Sue — applying for the Clerical Assistant job at Knolls Hill School.

First attempt
Well, I'm 35 and divorced with two children aged five and 12. I like being at home really but I need some extra money, so that is why I am looking for a job. My ex-husband does not pay me enough to keep the children. As you will see from my CV, I have recently taken a Word-Perfect course, to update my skills.

Comments
The first three sentences will not help Sue's cause. Her age is on her CV so there is no need to repeat it. Neither is there any need to mention the ages of children, unless asked. Saying that she does not particularly want to work anyway will put her prospective employer off, as will talk of her personal problems.

Second attempt
Well, I consider myself to be a mature and reliable person. Although I haven't worked for some years, I have been involved with administra-

tive duties for the PTA at our local school. I also took a WordPerfect course at a private college recently, in order to update my secretarial skills. At the moment I am working in a friend's secretarial bureau for a few hours each week and there I have learnt how to use a variety of office machinery and computer programs. During my time there I have discovered how much I enjoy being with other people. I would now like to take a permanent job where I can put my skills to good use and a school environment sounds very attractive to me.

Comments
This says all that is necessary without sounding too 'pushy'.

Mary — applying for the job as part-time general assistant at Lowprices Superstore.

First attempt
I'm 52 — a bit old really, I suppose. I've spent the last 12 years looking after my mother. She has just died so I would like a job again as I am going mad at home all day. I'm not very up with all the new technology although my friend showed me how to use a computerised till. I expect I could learn more things, but it takes me a long time to grasp anything new — it must be my age!

Comments
It is quite obvious from the above that Mary has a complex about her age and this will be immediately apparent to her interviewer too. Her negative attitude is unlikely to get her the job she so badly wants.

Second attempt
I used to work in our family shop for many years, until my mother became ill and I had to nurse her. Now that she has died I am anxious to get back to work again. I enjoy meeting people and like to think that I can get on with anyone. I have been working in my friend's shop recently in order to learn about computerised tills and other recent changes, so I feel I am now up to date. The job you are offering sounds interesting and varied, and I'm sure I could learn any duties that I am not already familiar with.

Comments
A much more positive attitude.

Richard — applying for a job as a computer operator. The interview has been arranged by the Jobcentre.

First attempt

I know you must think I am not employable with my past record, but I am planning on going straight now. I have a girlfriend and a child so I need some steady money coming in. I haven't got any experience as a computer operator, but I really like working with them.

Comments

This sounds honest, but a little negative. Richard should play up his good points rather than emphasise his bad ones.

Second attempt

You will have seen my prison record from my CV, but that is all behind me now. I was there for drug offences, rather than anything violent. I have never taken drugs myself, but foolishly handled them for a friend. I paid the price for my mistake. I'm looking forward to the future now though, and to supporting my partner and our child. While in prison I took several training courses using computers and I soon realised that they fascinated me. I have a computer at home which I use whenever I can. The job you are offering sounds as though it is just what I am looking for.

Comments

Richard sounds keen and eager to please. His prospective employer should feel from this that Richard is determined to hold down a responsible job, doing what he enjoys most which is working with computers.

Andrew — applying for a job as a sales rep. He has been told about this by a friend and thinks it sounds like fun.

First attempt

I've led a rather interesting life really. As you will see from my CV I haven't spent much time in England, but I have enjoyed myself moving from place to place. John, your rep for the Midlands, told me about this job and it sounds just right for me. I have a degree, you know, and I am sure I would be a valuable asset to your company.

Comments

Andrew is making himself sound extremely big-headed. He would not, from the above, give his prospective employer the impression that he is treating this job opportunity as a serious career move.

Second attempt
As you will see from my CV I have moved around quite a bit in the past, but I now want to settle down here in England. John, your Midlands rep, told me about this job and I must say it sounds very interesting. Although I obtained a degree, I have never put it to good use, and I feel this could be my opportunity to do so.

Comments
This gives the impression that Andrew does intend to settle down into a career and that he could prove to be a valuable employee.

CHECKLIST

- Have you checked the date and time of your interview?
- Do you know how long the journey will take?
- Have you acquired some background knowledge on the organisation in question?
- Have you chosen appropriate clothes to wear?
- Are you prepared to be asked awkward questions?
- Do you have some questions of your own to ask?
- Are you able to emphasise the benefits of your maturity?

POINTS FOR DISCUSSION

1   Do you think an interview situation gives a true impression of what a person is like?

2   How would you answer the following question: 'We really wanted someone younger for the job. If we did offer it to you how do you think you would cope at your age?'

3   You arrive late for an interview because your cat got run over just as you were leaving home. How would you explain your late arrival to your interviewer? What could you have done to help the situation?

9
Surviving the First Day

OVERCOMING PANIC

As the day gradually draws nearer to the start of your new job you will, no doubt, begin to feel both excited and apprehensive. Excited because you are, hopefully, looking forward to returning to the world of work and the challenges it offers you, but at the same time apprehensive about what lies ahead and in particular how you will cope on that first day.

Maybe you will not feel in the least bit panicky as you walk into your new place of work on the first morning. On the other hand, it is quite probable that you will. If your heart starts to beat at double speed and you feel like running in the opposite direction, take several slow, deep breaths, tell yourself that you are going to be all right, and that your feelings are quite normal. Keep walking in the right direction and, at the same time, start to put the situation into perspective.

What is the worst that can happen?
Suppose you make a complete idiot of yourself within the first few hours. Everything goes wrong. You blow up the new computer; no one talks to you and everyone falls about laughing hysterically every time you walk in the room. What would you do? You would, presumably, walk out vowing never to return. End of job and back to the newspaper ads or Jobcentre.

Now, even if all that were to happen, it wouldn't be the end of the world, would it? Surely not as serious as one of your children failing all their GCSEs, your partner breaking his/her leg, or your sister having an affair with the married man next door? No. So now you have the situation in perspective. If it all goes hopelessly wrong, you walk away and start again.

That is looking on the blackest side. In reality nothing untoward is likely to happen and you will be able to actually enjoy your first day and feel at the end of it that you made the right decision. You should also bear in mind that all your new colleagues are human beings too, with feelings just like yours. They will, no doubt, remember their first day and how they felt, so the chances are that they will go out of their way to make you feel at ease. You probably will make some mistakes, but that is to be expected. However brilliant you are, a new job needs to be learned and worked at and that cannot be done in the first half hour.

GETTING TO KNOW EVERYONE

Usually when you start a new job you will be met by a member of staff and introduced to your new colleagues. Smile at everyone in a friendly way and look as though you are pleased to be there. It is very important at this stage that you do not give the impression of being 'stuck up' or 'stand-offish'.

If you are hopeless at remembering names, jot down as many as you can after you have been introduced. It is unlikely, however, that anyone will get upset if you forget their name once or even twice. After that they may begin to get a little irritated!

Take your time to get to know your colleagues. The best plan to start with is to be friendly but not too friendly. First impressions of someone are not necessarily lasting ones. A good working relationship is what you are aiming for, but it often takes time to achieve this. Be especially wary of mixing business with pleasure — life can get very complicated and unpleasant should the situation get out of hand.

Here is a suggested plan for getting to know everyone:

- Always act in a friendly way
- Look at people as they speak to you
- Never let yourself seem bigheaded
- Try not to rush relationships
- Do not get upset if you seem to be left out at first
- Make allowances for other people's problems
- Do not treat people junior to you as inferior beings
- Offer to make the tea/coffee without waiting to be asked.

ASKING QUESTIONS AND LISTENING CAREFULLY

As long as they are relevant, your work colleagues are going to expect you to ask questions both on your first day and for several weeks after.

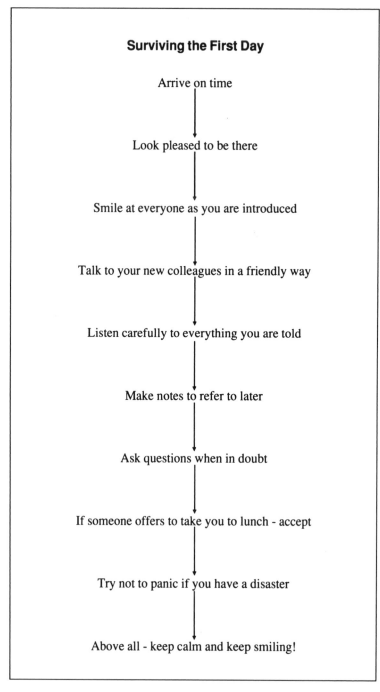

Surviving the First Day

Arrive on time

Look pleased to be there

Smile at everyone as you are introduced

Talk to your new colleagues in a friendly way

Listen carefully to everything you are told

Make notes to refer to later

Ask questions when in doubt

If someone offers to take you to lunch - accept

Try not to panic if you have a disaster

Above all - keep calm and keep smiling!

Fig. 9. Surviving the first day — a step-by-step guide.

There is no need for you to feel a nuisance. It is obviously important for you not to interrupt them when they are busy, but as long as you pick your moments, asking questions is one of the best ways to learn.

There is no point, however, in asking questions unless you are prepared to listen to the answers you are given. Listening is an art that many of us have not quite perfected. Firing question after question at a colleague without giving yourself the chance to digest the answers will be of little long term benefit. Ask one question at a time and, if necessary, make notes as the answer is given to you. Only ask the next question if you are sure it is still necessary.

Although no one should mind you asking questions, it hardly needs to be said that your colleagues will begin to mind if you ask those same questions again and again, just because you did not listen carefully enough the first time.

It is a good idea to use your listening skills, as well as your eyes, to observe what goes on around you. Although you should not, of course, listen in on private conversations, just listening to the day-to-day working talk between your colleagues can help to give you a good insight into the working environment you have joined.

ADOPTING THE RIGHT ATTITUDE

Your new colleagues will, quite understandably, only treat you decently if you do the same to them. If you adopt a cocky 'know it all' attitude they will have little time for you.

It is always the young who are said to have an 'attitude problem'. It is true that most young people do go through a phase where they treat everyone apart from their own friends with contempt and bored indifference. However, many mature adults have attitude problems too and returners to work are no exception.

Perhaps, for instance, you are returning to the same type of work that you did before, but in a lower position. It will be very tempting for you to try and tell everyone else, including your superiors, that you know how things should be done. This will not go down at all well. Your working days will be far better spent doing the job you have been employed to do, whilst at the same time taking the opportunity to get back into the swing of working life.

Very soon, with the right attitude, you will probably have the chance to work your way back up the ladder again anyway. Who knows — you may eventually reach a higher position than the one you held before your break from work.

Taking orders from younger staff

It is very likely that when you return to work you will have to take orders from a manager/boss/superior younger than yourself. Because they are younger does not mean that they are no good at their job. Age and ability are not necessarily linked at all, and everyone needs to be treated as an individual. Give them a chance. Do as they ask and do it to the best of your ability. Try not to resent their youth and apparent lack of worldly experience. They may appear to be arrogant and dynamic, but they will have been brought up and educated in a different way to you and, as a result, they now work in a different way too. Accept it from day one and you will do yourself a big favour.

THINKING POSITIVELY

At the end of your first day look back on your achievements. You will have begun to learn all about your new job and what it involves. At the same time, you will have met some new colleagues. But most important of all, you will have taken that first big step of facing up to the working world once more. No doubt you will feel tired by the time you arrive home, but as long as you are looking forward to day two, the tiredness will be in a good cause.

Think about your future in a positive way. On day two you can learn some more about your job, get to know your colleagues better and start to feel more familiar with your surroundings. By the end of the first week you should begin to feel part of your new organisation, and by the end of the first month you will probably have forgotten what it was like *not* to work.

CASE STUDIES

Sue

Sue gets the job at Knolls Hill School and on her first morning the Headteacher introduces her to the other teachers and staff by calling them all together in the staff room. Sue feels very self-conscious about all the attention she is given, but everyone seems very friendly, apart from one lady, who turns out to be one of the housemistresses.

This particular lady says hello to Sue but does not offer to shake her hand and just walks out of the staff room afterwards. Sue wonders why she is acting this way, until the other clerical assistant tells her that Mary, the housemistress, wanted Sue's job when it became vacant and that she resents Sue for getting it instead.

Rather than get upset about her attitude, Sue goes to see Mary straight away and tells her that she is sorry about the situation, but that she hopes they can still be friends. After all it is not Sue's fault that she was offered the job rather than Mary. Mary seems to appreciate Sue's frankness and even invites her to lunch.

Sue is determined to get on with all her colleagues, and they in turn respect her for the stand she has taken with Mary. Day one ends on a cheerful note and Sue goes home looking forward to the following day.

Mary

Mary is offered the job at Lowprices Superstore and she accepts, thrilled that she will be working once again. She is really keen to learn everything and on her first day she works with one of the other ladies on the checkout. She makes notes of all she is told and by the end of the day she is able to operate the till herself with the other lady supervising.

Mary already knows several of the other ladies who work there and she feels that she will very soon settle in to her new environment.

Richard

Richard came over very well at his interview and Dingleside Company Products decide to take him on as a computer operator for a three month trial period. Richard feels it is fair of them to insist on the trial period in the circumstances.

On his first morning Richard is introduced to his four male colleagues by their manager. They all eye him up rather suspiciously, having been told his past record. Richard smiles at them all and pretends he has not noticed their suspicious looks. He listens carefully while his new manager begins to explain the job to him.

At lunchtime, one of the others asks Richard if he would like to go with them to the canteen. Richard is pleased that they are, after all, going to give him a chance and he accepts gratefully. He knows he now has the opportunity to prove to himself and his family that he can make a fresh start and he is determined to succeed.

Andrew

Mainly because of his friend's influence, Andrew is offered a junior sales rep position. He is a little peeved at the 'junior' title at his age, but he supposes he will have to start somewhere. In any case he knows that in no time he will be able to tell them what to do and then he will be promoted.

For the first day, Andrew goes out on the road with one of the other reps. Tom is very experienced, having worked in the company for 15 years. He is well qualified to explain the job to Andrew, but he is immediately put off by Andrew's cocky attitude. By the end of the day Tom has had enough and tells the area manager that he is not prepared to take Andrew out again.

CHECKLIST

- Have you managed to get your panic feelings under control?
- Can you put the importance of the job into perspective?
- Are you prepared to be friendly to your new colleagues?
- Have you adopted the right attitude?
- Are you ready to listen to what you are told about the job?
- Have you bothered to make notes to refer to later?
- Can you think positively about your future at work?
- Are you now sure that returning to work was the right choice to make?

POINTS FOR DISCUSSION

1   Supposing it was your first day in a new office. What would you do if everyone completely ignored you?

2   You are returning to your old company, to do what you thought was your old job. When you start, however, you discover that your job has been downgraded and a man several years younger than you is now effectively in charge of what was your department. How would you cope with this situation?

3   Devise a list of guidelines for employers to work from, so that new staff are made to feel welcome and at ease.

10
Setting up Your Own Business

THINKING ABOUT SETTING UP ON YOUR OWN

There are certain myths to be dispelled about running your own business. Firstly, it is **not** an easy option, although it might seem to be so. Secondly, it is said by many that working for yourself is the best and quickest way to make a lot of money, far more money than can be made in most employed positions. Unfortunately, although this can be true, it is also one of the quickest ways to lose a lot of money, unless sufficient planning and research are undertaken at the outset. Thirdly, contrary to popular opinion, when you work for yourself you cannot just work when you feel like it, otherwise very soon you will have no business at all. You are your own boss, it is true, but you are still restricted by the demands of others.

Many new businesses are born through circumstance rather than choice. With the job situation as it stands today there seem to be fewer vacancies around to be filled. Many people see setting themselves up in their own business as the only way that they will be able to work again following redundancy or a break from work.

If you are thinking about setting up a business you should generally be:

- in good health
- clear about what you want to do
- capable of working on your own or with your partner if you have one
- self motivating and tough
- the type who doesn't make impulsive decisions
- able to get on with other people
- determined to succeed
- able to work under pressure
- in a position to put the business first when necessary
- courageous enough to continue when the going gets tough.

The personal satisfaction to be gained from setting up a successful business can make many of the hassles along the way seem quite incidental, but that is only when the business is a success. Many small businesses fail almost before they begin, for reasons that we shall look at later on.

To sum up, the rewards from self employment can be many, but you must be prepared to make a total commitment to your business if it is to flourish.

CONSIDERING YOUR OPTIONS AND YOUR ASSETS

In order to set some ideas in motion, write down the following headings:

- What experience have you got?
- What are you particularly interested in doing? (This could be a hobby.)
- What contacts do you have?
- What financial assets do you have to help you to set up your business?
- Do you have friends or family who would run the business with you?

Write down as much information as you possibly can under each heading. You will also need to give some thought at this point as to whether you intend to go it alone or set up with a partner.

Perhaps your most important asset, and that of any partner you may work with, is 'stickability'. Businesses are not built up overnight and if you are going to get demoralised and upset every time you suffer a setback, you should not be thinking about self employment. You will not make much money at first, and you will have to put long hours into building up your business. You have to be determined to succeed, whatever personal sacrifices are necessary. Business sense can be learned as you go along, but only if you are the right type to be starting the business in the first place.

RESEARCHING THE MARKET AND FACING THE FACTS

Having decided what you are good at and possibly also what you would like to be good at, you can then start to think more seriously about actual business ideas. There are two main types of business ideas:

1   Those that build on other people's concepts

2   Those that are entirely new *ie*, where you do not know of anyone doing anything similar.

Your immediate feeling may be that you should try something completely new. You should, however, be wary of doing this. It is just possible that your idea is a brilliant one in a completely untapped market, but it is also possible that a market does not exist and that is why no one has succeeded before you.

On the other hand, where there is competition there is a market, so never be afraid of starting a similar business to someone else. You just have to make sure that yours is better!

Why businesses fail

Small businesses can fail for many reasons:

- Because the market for the business has **not been properly researched**. In other words, there is not sufficient demand for what you have to offer to provide the necessary amount of money for the business to survive. Perhaps the market is already saturated or perhaps it just does not exist.

- Because the business is **under-funded**. So many people start a business on a shoe-string. Shops open with virtually no stock. Offices are set up with very little equipment etc. If you are setting up a new business you need sufficient money behind you to buy stock/equipment and to rent or buy suitable premises if you are not working from home. You also need to be able to live for the first year or so, when very little money, if any, will be coming in. Taking out a hefty loan might solve the problem in the short term, but that loan has to be repaid each month.

- Because **the money isn't handled properly**. Lavish unnecessary equipment, fancy cars, ads on TV and expensive business lunches must wait until the business starts to show a profit.

- Because of a **lack of advertising** before the business starts and during its operation.

Making sure that there is a viable market for the business you intend to start is vitally important. Whilst competition is a good thing, opening a greengrocer's shop in a town that already contains ten greengrocers does not make a lot of sense. But people still seem to do it. Similarly, starting a business selling expensive, top of the range cars in a poverty stricken area of the country doesn't make much economic sense either, but again someone somewhere will give it a try.

The research you need to do into whether or not a viable market exists for your product or service will vary according to what sort of business you are considering. If, for instance you are going to make parts for bicycles which you plan to sell direct to other companies, you should contact them first to see if they would be interested in buying from you. If you plan to open a shop, you should check to see how many other shops there are in your area selling what you intend to sell. If you fancy becoming a window cleaner and have a particular area in mind, you will need to know whether someone else is already covering that area.

So every different type of business will require different market research, but it is very important that this research is carried out properly before committing yourself to anything. There has to be a need for what you are going to offer, otherwise your business stands no chance of surviving, however much effort you put into it.

RAISING THE FINANCE

How much start-up finance you will need obviously depends on the type of business you envisage. Some home-based businesses, such as typing services, telesales work etc, will take very little capital to set up. On the other hand, a large-scale operation involving the renting or buying of large, prestige premises, the hiring of several staff and substantial equipment to be leased or bought is entirely a different matter.

It is possible to join the Government's **Business Start Up Scheme**, whereby you will receive a small cash payment each week for 40 weeks, but this will not actually help you to set up the business. If you do not have funds available to use you will have to take out a loan of some kind. One option is to **re-mortgage** your house, thus releasing some capital for your new venture. Another option is to approach one of the high street banks and ask them for a **business loan**.

A word of warning with regard to any loan you may take out. Be very careful not to borrow too much. Loan payments can cripple small businesses. Interest rates can vary and what seemed at one time a fairly realistic monthly repayment can suddenly become a far higher one. If nearly all the money you take in immediately goes out again to repay your loan, your future will not be very secure, to say the least. An accountant or bank manager will advise you on how much you can safely borrow.

In addition, a bank will require a sound business plan, prepared by yourself and/or an accountant, before they will consider lending you any money. A business plan should show:

- what you intend to do
- where you intend to do it
- why you think your idea is a good one
- your current financial position
- a forecast of the money you expect to come in during, say, the first year
- how much you want to borrow.

GETTING OFF THE GROUND

Once you have decided what business you are going to start, how you intend to fund it, and where the premises are to be, you will be ready to think about beginning to trade.

As far as premises are concerned, if you are intending to run your business from home, remember to check on your house deeds to make sure that you are allowed to do so. It is also worth making a 'phone call to your local council, as in some cases **planning permission** might be needed if you wish to use part of your home as your business on a permanent basis. If you are renting or buying premises elsewhere, check whether you need to notify the council of a 'change of use'. You should be quite sure that you can trade from your chosen premises before actually starting the business.

You will need to think of a name for your business and have some stationery printed. You may need signs made for a shopfront or to hang outside your office. Furniture, equipment and stock will have to be purchased. The list of what to do will obviously vary according to the business you are starting, but you are going to be spending a very busy time, that much is sure!

One major reason why businesses fail is due to lack of **advertising**. If no one knows that you exist they will not be able to do business with you. It is vitally important to advertise well in advance of starting your business, so that you can begin to build up some trade straight away.

For example, if you are planning to open a greengrocer's shop in your local town, you could advertise in the local newspaper and perhaps also send out leaflets to individual houses. If you are starting a business where you are selling direct to companies, you would be well advised to send individual letters to those companies so that they know all about you and what you intend to do. *Yellow Pages* is a good place to advertise too, although this is obviously more of a long-term plan as the book is unlikely to be reprinted to coincide with your opening!

Depending on what you are planning to do, you might decide to hold a 'grand opening'. Taking the greengrocer's shop as an example again, perhaps special opening offers and free gifts on the first day could be the way to attract potential customers. Competition is likely to be tough, whatever business you start, and people do get taken in by gimmicks. Your products or services have got to be consistently good after the opening attractions, however: substandard goods will not fool the public for long and they will soon revert to their original suppliers.

Make sure that your immediate family and friends know that the first few months are going to be tough going and you might not be able to spend as much time with them as you would like. If you have explained this in advance, and they say they understand, then you will not feel so guilty every time you have to work late or give up a precious Sunday to sort out a business problem.

Once your business is finally off the ground, you can begin to look forward to the months and years ahead, hard work though they may be. Hopefully, if you have done your homework, your business will be a success and you will feel a great sense of achievement, reaping the rewards of what you have created.

CASE STUDIES

Paula

Paula has managed to find a rambling old house in the town centre. She has applied to the council for change of use, as at the moment it is a private house, although they have told her that there should not be a problem. Her husband is still not convinced that it is a good idea, but Paula will be providing some of the funding from money left to her by her parents, so he cannot really say too much.

Paula has asked her bank to lend her some money for equipping the nursing home. They have agreed, although she did have to provide them with some projected figures and a sound business plan.

Once the planning and financial side have been sorted out, Paula begins to advertise. She needs to advertise the nursing home to potential clients, and she also needs to advertise for staff to run the home. Her plan is to open the home approximately three months after the first batch of advertising, providing she can fill ten of the 20 places on offer. She is sure that she will have no problems recruiting staff as job vacancies are few and far between in their area, and she is sure people will jump at the chance to work for her.

Six months after finding the premises, The Greengables Nursing Home opens amid a blaze of publicity. A well known MP opens the home and already Paula has her ten expected places filled with four more on offer. The only problem is that she is short of staff. Paula has become fairly well known in the area and she is considered to be a big snob. A lot of the locals are reluctant to work for her. In the end she is forced to take on some rather unsuitable staff in order to be able to open at all.

John

John has decided to start in a very small way, running his business from home. He has checked on his house deeds and there seem to be no problems there. He has also telephoned the council, but as he only intends to use his dining room on a part-time basis for his business, they do not foresee any objections from neighbours.

John puts a small advert in the local paper and starts to teach on an individual basis. He starts with only a few clients, but he hopes that this will build up once he gets known in the area.

CHECKLIST

- Have you thought about why you want to set up your own business?
- Do you think you are the right sort of person to be self employed?
- Have you got 'stickability'?
- Can you cope with pressure?
- What are you good at doing?
- Do you think you have a viable business idea?
- Will there be a market for it?
- What about premises?
- Can you raise the necessary cash to get you started?
- Have you got a sound business plan?
- Are you doing sufficient advertising?
- Is your business going to begin in a positive way?

POINTS FOR DISCUSSION

1   Write down what you see as the advantages and disadvantages of self employment.

2   Do you think there will be more or fewer self employed people in say 5 years' time? Give reasons for your answer.

3   'Self employment means you can work when you want to.' Do you see this statement as true or false? State why.

11
Running Your Business Successfully

KEEPING ACCURATE RECORDS

For many people running a business, the paperwork can prove to be a headache. This does not have to be the case, however, so long as you are organised right from the start.

Although some might consider it an extravagance, it is generally well worth using an **accountant** for your end of year accounts. For what is a comparatively small amount each year your accounts will be properly prepared for the Inland Revenue, and your accountant is likely to know exactly what you can claim as legitimate expenses, possibly saving you money in the long run. He or she will also tell you what records you should keep and how to keep them.

For many small businesses a simple **cash book** can be used to record all receipts and payments. As long as this is kept up to date on a daily or weekly basis, the accounts will not get out of hand.

Recording transactions

It is very important to record all transactions so that you can keep control. You need to know what it is costing you to run your business so that you know whether you are charging the correct price for your goods and/or services. Fixed costs, such as rent, rates and salaries, should be recorded along with variable costs such as petrol, advertising etc. Always remember that being busier does not necessarily mean you are earning more money. If you have underpriced your goods or services you will not make a profit.

Invoices, statements etc, should be sent out to customers promptly, stating the date by which you require payment. 30 days is the usual time. If payment is not received by that date, send a chasing letter and if necessary another, until you receive your money.

Quite apart from recording all transactions for control of the business, you will also need to know your receipts, payments and resultant profit or loss figure in order to complete your annual tax return.

You and the taxman

When you start your business you should inform:

- your local Inspector of Taxes with regard to paying tax
- your local Department of Social Security with regard to National Insurance contributions.

As a self employed person you are liable to pay **income tax** on part of your earnings, assuming the income you obtain from working for yourself exceeds your allowances. (You can earn a certain amount of money each year without being liable for tax. This amount is known as your personal allowance.)

For a small business a Profit and Loss Account showing gross earnings, the legitimate expenses incurred in the running of the business and the net profit achieved should be enough to satisfy the tax authorities. Income tax is charged on the taxable profits in your business usually over a 12 month period. Your year does not have to run from January to December. It will usually start when your business begins trading for the very first time.

If your earnings are over a certain figure you will also be liable to pay Class 2 **National Insurance** contributions as a weekly flat rate payment. In addition, you may have to pay Class 4 contributions which are calculated as a percentage of your profits.

When and if your business is looking as though it is likely to achieve a turnover close to the **VAT** (Value Added Tax) threshold, you should register for VAT on a form provided by your local Customs and Excise Office. You will then be given a VAT number which has to be printed on all business stationery. If in any doubt whether or not you need to register, contact your local Customs and Excise Office for advice.

ESTABLISHING A ROUTINE

A satisfactory day to day routine needs to be established if your business is to flourish. If a customer telephones querying an item on an order, you must be able to find a copy of that order straight away. In the same way, a business client sitting waiting for you in a hotel, where you have agreed to meet for lunch, will not be very impressed if you forget all about the appointment!

The following measures will help you to establish an efficiently run business:

Use a diary
Whenever you make an appointment or need to be reminded to carry out a certain task on a certain day, write the details down in a diary and refer to that diary every single day. Never rely on your memory. One day it will let you down.

Maintain an adequate filing system
A paper mountain with weeks and weeks of correspondence, bills etc, will not aid your business. Start a simple filing system which is suitable for your needs and file everything in it. If correspondence needs to be acted on at a later date, place it in a pending file, and refer to that file on a daily basis. Filing is not nearly as bad as everyone makes out, just so long as it is done regularly.

Keep a 'Jobs to be done' list
What you write on such a list will obviously depend on the type of business you are running. If, for instance, you run a garden centre and every so often you have to check the stock just to make sure it is still alive, make a note of what you need to look at and when, so that you can firstly remind yourself to do the check, and secondly tick off that task from your list when it is done.

A highly organised person is far more likely to succeed in business. If half a day is spent looking for information which should be readily available, then valuable time is lost, time which you cannot afford to lose. Time is money when you work for yourself.

BELIEVING IN YOUR ABILITY

Believing in yourself is even more important in your own business than it is when you work for someone else. After all, if you are not sure about your ability to succeed no one else is likely to feel encouraged to try your goods or services, because your negative attitude will come across.

Of course, if you are offering the very best in the way of goods or services, then you are going to find it fairly easy to believe that you will succeed. For this reason, you should always feel that you are producing your very best.

Whatever business you are in, even when the initial hurdles are overcome, there will still be times when business is bad, and you must be prepared for such eventualities. You just have to stick it out, hoping that things will improve, and giving the best possible service to those customers you do have. Tell yourself that your fortunes will change and that when that time comes you will be ready to move forward and so adapt to the increased business activity.

When times are good and you are making lots of money, you should resist the temptation to spend it all. Instead, try to build up a reserve fund for when times get bad again, as they invariably will. That way you will be able to ride the highs and lows without too much variation in your living standards!

BUILDING UP A REPUTATION

When you first set up your business you will have to rely almost entirely on coverage in newspapers or other forms of advertising in order to tell people that you exist and what you are able to offer. Once you become established, your aim is to attract new customers by personal recommendation, which costs you nothing. Personal recommendation is the best form of advertising there is, not only because it is free, but also because it means that you have been accepted and approved by your customers.

Personal recommendation is not, however, a right. You will only be recommended if you provide the relevant goods or services in a satisfactory manner. You have to keep your customers happy. If you upset someone you will not just lose their business. They will talk to others and the resultant gossip may well seriously damage your business.

What happens in the day to day running of your business is entirely up to you and — if you have one — your partner. Unlike in a large organisation where many people may be responsible for a business transaction you are not going to be able to pass on the blame for anything that goes wrong.

In order to build up your reputation, remember the following:

- Give thought and sympathy to your customers' emotional needs. They may seem to you to be making petty demands or acting in an unnecessarily anxious fashion but you just have to grin and bear it.

- Return telephone calls promptly, especially if messages have been left on an answerphone.

- Make sure you are always polite, whether you are speaking to customers face to face, on the telephone, or sending them a letter.

- Do not turn work away unless you absolutely have to. That customer might go somewhere else — permanently!

In order to survive in the tough small business world of today, you must be able to provide goods/services to an extremely high standard, and you must also treat your customers as special people. After all they are providing your livelihood so they are very special indeed!

EXPANDING THE BUSINESS

The first thing to say about expanding your business is DON'T, until you are sure that the time is right. There is a saying that 'small is beautiful' and this can apply to businesses in much the same way as anything else. Many businesses that survived very well with just one, two or three people involved, have folded when their owners decided to expand.

When, and if, you do feel that you are ready to expand your business, give serious thought to how you want to do it. Do you want to open another branch? Do you want to employ more staff in your present outlet? Do you want to increase your range of products/services? All these questions should be answered and a good deal of research carried out before any expansion takes place.

Expansion usually requires money, and unless you have the resources yourself you will have to approach a bank or some other financial institution and ask them for a loan. In the same way as when you started your business, you will need to provide them with a business plan, saying how you want to expand, why you think it is necessary, and how the project is to be financed. You will also need to supply business accounts showing your present turnover and profit.

Contrary to what some people seem to think, banks and other lenders are unlikely to lend you money to expand unless your present business is showing some signs of success. In other words, they are unlikely to throw good money after bad.

CASE STUDIES

John
John advertised in the local paper at first, but he now finds that his

reputation is growing through word of mouth. All of a sudden he is inundated with enquiries and his part-time work soon starts to stretch into a full-time occupation. At this point he decides to look around for a small office, as he is worried about what the neighbours think about the steady stream of callers to their house.

Eventually John finds a small office — just one room, plus the use of a toilet and kitchen — for a reasonable rent. Although by now he is operating a waiting list, he does not intend to employ anyone as he wants to know that everyone receives the same standard of tuition. He also feels that while he is working on his own all the profits will be his, rather than shared.

Because he is on his own, John is able to fit all his hours around the children. He begins working for three evenings a week when his partner is at home to babysit, and their lifestyle soon takes an upward turn with his earnings to boost the household's income.

Paula

Paula has plenty of clients, but she still cannot find all the staff she needs. Complaints start to be made and her newly found business begins to suffer, with relatives threatening to take their loved ones away unless more qualified staff are employed right away.

Because of her self inflicted reputation Paula has not been able to recruit many locals. She is therefore forced to advertise for staff from other areas, offering them accommodation and high salaries in order to get what she needs.

Eventually, by the end of the first year, Greengables is running on an even keel, as far as staff and clients are concerned, and Paula breathes a sigh of relief. Her only problem now is that the business is not yet running at a profit and she is finding it hard to meet the loan repayments. She knows, however, that until the remaining six places are filled she will have to be content with what is coming in. She has learned the hard way that reputation has to be earned and at long last is beginning to realise that running a business of her own is not nearly as easy as she thought it would be.

CHECKLIST

- Are you keeping accurate records of all receipts and payments?

- Have you told the relevant authorities about your business?

- Are you likely to reach the VAT threshold? If so, have you applied for VAT registration?

- Is your business beginning to attract people through personal recommendation?

- Are you giving a good service to your customers?

- Have you established an effective day to day routine?

- Do you consider that you are well organised?

- Is it the right time to expand your business?

- Are you sure that the risks involved in expansion will pay off?

- Are you prepared for the 'lows' as well as the 'highs' involved in working for yourself, and do you have a reserve fund to see you through?

POINTS FOR DISCUSSION

1   'Personal recommendation is the best form of advertising.' Discuss this statement.

2   Discuss the advantages and disadvantages of working with a partner rather than alone.

3   Assume you are working alone in a catering business, supplying pubs and restaurants with speciality ice cream. You have plenty of work, but a very well known chain of restaurants asks you to supply them too. Would you turn the business down and, if not, how would you handle the situation?

12
Organising Your New Life

DOING HOUSEHOLD CHORES

Perhaps this section affects women rather than men, although in our so-called equal society there are probably some men who are responsible for the everyday running of the home.

Returning to work means a drastic change in your domestic routine. The running of the home has to revolve around your working hours, and it is up to you to utilise your time in the best way possible.

Surprisingly enough, many people find they actually get more done when they have less time to do it in. If you have all day to think about cleaning the house, the chances are you will leave it till the last possible moment to start - when you can't possibly manage any more cups of coffee or depressing pages of the daily paper! On the other hand, if you only have Saturday morning available, then Saturday morning it has to be.

You will probably have to come to terms with the fact that your high standards may have to be compromised. Perhaps you are not too fussy over housework anyway, but if you are you will just have to accept that you no longer have the time to empty out the contents of the kitchen cupboards every week, or to hoover every time someone visits. Similarly, if you are used to cooking gourmet meals from scratch, you may find you need to resort to frozen chicken pies and oven chips rather more often than before.

Does it matter? The chances are that no-one will notice any difference. In fact the family will probably enjoy the convenience foods and feel more comfortable in the 'lived in' house.

If you really cannot accept a drop in standards or feel that you just do not have any free time to devote to your home, you could perhaps consider taking on someone to help you, perhaps with the cleaning, or with the cooking. This is not admitting defeat, just helping you to cope with your new working responsibilities.

KEEPING UP YOUR SOCIAL LIFE

When you start in a new job, changing your whole lifestyle in the process, there is a temptation to give up a lot of your leisure commitments, so that you have more free time. If possible, resist this temptation. Your social life is as important as your working life. Apart from being with your friends, your social life will help you to relax and recover from the stresses and strains of working life.

Many organisations have social clubs for their employees. These clubs may take the form of a bar, perhaps with entertainment, and/or various sporting facilities. In addition, staff outings to places of interest may be arranged from time to time. It is up to you to decide how much you intend to become a part of such merrymaking. Many people do not like to mix business with pleasure; on the other hand, some people's working and social lives become entwined and that is how they like it. Every individual is different.

Try to keep work and your home life in separate compartments. There is nothing more boring for other people than listening to a blow by blow account of your day at work, when you are all out for a pleasant, relaxing evening. Brief chats about work between a group can be interesting and informative, but if the conversation centres around just one person and what has happened to them that day, then everyone will soon be yawning and want to go home.

FINDING TIME FOR YOURSELF

However much you love your partner or your family, you are bound to want to spend some time on your own, doing just what you feel like doing. There is nothing at all wrong with this. The problem arises when there just does not seem to be any time left for you after you have seen to the needs of everyone else. What you have to realise is that you deserve your space too.

By organising yourself properly, you should be able to set aside at least a couple of hours a week just for you. That time may be spent reading, watching television, having a bath, or doing absolutely nothing. Perhaps you will decide to go shopping and spoil yourself by buying something that you could not afford if you were not working. The whole point is that you should decide what you want to do and just go and do it, without stopping to consider everyone else.

COPING WITH FEELING TIRED

Tiredness is an occupational hazard when you start a new job. After all, not only are you coping with getting used to the actual hours out at work, plus the travelling time involved, you are also learning the job, with all the necessary concentration involved.

The obvious answer to feeling tired is to make sure that you have enough sleep, particularly during the first few weeks back at work. Go to bed at a reasonable time each night, preferably after a relaxing hot drink and bath. Read in bed for a while if that seems to help you get off to sleep. If you wake up in the middle of the night worrying about the next day at work, try to tell yourself that you will cope with that next day when it arrives and then turn over and go back to sleep!

Due to the drastic changes in your life you might find it difficult to sleep peacefully every night for the first few weeks. If so, get hold of a copy of one of the many books available on relaxation. Practise a few exercises during the evening and see if they help.

Sleeping in on your days off will help you to catch up on any lost sleep. But don't worry too much about occasional insomnia. Once your life settles down into a routine, so your sleeping patterns will adjust and settle down too.

AVOIDING STRESS

'Stress' seems to be a very fashionable word today. Some kinds of stress are said to be good and other kinds of stress are said to be bad. So what exactly do we mean by the word 'stress'? The dictionary gives the definitions: tension, strain, pressure. Three more words that seem to crop up frequently in our everyday lives.

Some people, on the surface at least, seem to perform better under stress. The only problem is that although they may perform well, they may at the same time be putting their physical well-being at risk. Too much stress can cause all kinds of physical and psychological ailments.

Although it is easy to say and hard to carry out, you should always try to take life as it comes, without getting tense or anxious every time something goes wrong. Keep your problems in perspective. Look at other people and you will probably see that they have far more problems than you.

Starting a new job is bound to be a stressful time, but you can do yourself a good turn by telling yourself that you can only do your best, and if that is not good enough perhaps the job is not right for you after all. Don't be afraid to admit to making mistakes. No one is going to mind if you tell them about an error. They will mind far more if you try to cover it up.

Most importantly, do not take on too much too soon. One of the biggest causes of job-related stress is overwork. If you feel constantly under pressure, pressure that is becoming too much for you, then tell someone or think about changing your job. In the same way, if you feel you are doing work that one of your colleagues should be doing, say so. There is no reason at all why you should be expected to do their job too.

Reducing your stress levels

The following tips may help you to reduce your stress levels at work:

- Discuss any work problems you have, either with your boss or with a partner/friend.

- If you are expected to take on a new task, ask to be trained first.

- Never be afraid to delegate some of your duties if you are in a position to do so.

- Take regular exercise and eat properly. Do not skip lunch breaks.

- Plan your days off so that you have something to look forward to.

- If you do feel under stress, practise relaxation techniques. You will find a variety of books which offer advice on this.

Remember that however good you, or others, think you are at your job, no one is indispensable. Making yourself ill is just not worth it. Life is too short anyway without increasing your chances of an early heart attack.

Relaxing in your leisure hours, spending time laughing and joking with others, pursuing hobbies such as sport, painting, golf etc, will all help to counteract stress. It is worth spending some time finding out what relaxes you most.

CASE STUDIES

Sue

Sue settles in to life at Knolls Hill School very well. She has managed to find an elderly lady to look after the children any time they are ill. The same lady offers to babysit any evening that Sue decides to go out.

Now that Sue is mixing with the outside world again at work, she decides to try increasing her social life too. She joins an evening class in conversational French and soon begins to really enjoy her Monday evenings out.

After a couple of months at the class, Sue becomes friendly with one of the male students and they begin having a drink together after classes. He too is divorced and neither of them want to get involved with anyone too soon, so their friendship is purely platonic, but Sue enjoys the chats they have and feels relaxed in his company.

Mary

Mary too is settling in well to her new job. As she works part-time she is still able to fit her housework and other chores around her working hours, and she buys all her food from Lowprices, so she does not have to make a special journey to the supermarket.

Mary has always set herself very high standards at home. She enjoys cooking and housework, and she is determined that her standards will be maintained. As a result she does get rather tired and her husband tries to get her to slow down a little.

In the end they reach a compromise. Mary's husband helps her to clean the house properly once a week, and in between Mary just pops round with the hoover and duster as necessary. She begins to experiment with a few convenience foods too, and they discover they rather enjoy the change.

Richard

Richard reaches the end of his three month trial and is offered the job on a permanent basis. He is thrilled to be working at something he enjoys so much and he does not get the time to even consider reverting to his previous ways.

He joins the social club attached to the company and he and his girlfriend go there on a Saturday evening, while her mother babysits. He becomes popular with the other staff, as he likes a good time and never minds buying a round for them all. For the first time in his life he feels settled.

Andrew

Life is not proving at all easy for Andrew. After the other rep, Tom, refused to go out on the road with him again, the area manager calls Andrew into his office and explains a few facts of life.

He reminds Andrew that he has been taken on as a junior rep, and that until such a time as he is promoted, he will take his orders from those more senior to him in status if not in age. The area manager says that Andrew's cocky attitude will not be tolerated by him or any of his colleagues and that it is up to him to change this attitude or leave the company.

Andrew gives all this serious thought. He knows he needs the job and he decides to play their game and do his work as well as he can. He gets very frustrated with life in general at times and has to keep reminding himself that in time he will get promoted, if he does as he is told.

John

John has to establish a very strict routine in order to fulfil his househusband duties as well as his teaching commitments. He manages to juggle the two quite well most of the time, but every now and then things get out of hand and he begins to feel very tense and under too much pressure. When this happens he tries to work in a few hours to himself and he takes himself off fishing, a sport he has just discovered.

He gets very tired, but then so does his partner, so they try to get to bed early during the week and, if the children will let them, they have a lie in at weekends. John knows that he must resist the temptation to take on too many hours, otherwise his teaching standards will drop through lack of time for preparation and marking.

Paula

Paula gets worked up very easily and she feels constantly under stress. She tends to be very dramatic about minor incidents and ends up with a splitting headache when anything goes wrong. Her husband gives his professional opinion that she is trying to do too much on her own, and on his recommendation she takes on a Matron to help her with the running of the home.

For the first year Paula and her husband do not go out together at all as she never seems to be home, and he begins to get very cross about their lack of social life. In the end he insists that she takes evenings off so that they can go out occasionally and she can spend some time with their son, who is growing fast.

CHECKLIST

● Have you established a routine for your home life?
● Can you accept that you will not have as much time as you did before you went back to work?

- Do you still have an active social life?
- Can you manage to sneak a few hours a week to yourself?
- Are you getting enough sleep?
- Do you feel stressed and, if so, what do you intend to do about it?
- Are you finding time for relaxation, exercise and proper food?

POINTS FOR DISCUSSION

1 Why do you think stress plays such a major part in our lives today?

2 List as many ways as you can think of to avoid stress both at home and at work?

3 If your partner brought home work to do every evening and talked about his/her job all the time, what would you say and do about it?

13
Handling the Family

CONSIDERING YOUR PARTNER

There you are, elated about your super new job, re-living every single minute, yet your partner just does not seem to understand your enthusiasm. In fact, he or she shows definite lack of interest when you relate, for the fourth time, how you were told at the end of the first week that they did not know how they had ever managed without you. How selfish not to want to listen, you might be thinking, but wait a minute, put yourself in your partner's shoes. How would you like to be on the receiving end? The chances are that you would soon get bored too.

By all means talk to your partner about your new job, but get to know when to stop and also be prepared to listen to details of your partner's day. The two of you should be able to have amicable discussions, not only about work, but about the rest of your lives as well. Relaxing in the evening, chatting over a bottle of wine, is a very enjoyable way to spend your leisure time, but keep the conversation stimulating, rather than a boring recital about who said what to whom and why they said it.

If you work together in your own business, then avoiding work as the main topic of conversation is even more important, otherwise neither of you will ever feel relaxed and able to get on with your home life.

Maintaining a good relationship
In order to maintain good relationships with your partner:

- choose your time to discuss any problems you may have at work
- consider his or her feelings and problems too
- set aside definite times to spend together
- do not shut your partner out of your life by working too many hours and consequently always feeling tired at home

- try, whenever possible, to leave work behind when you come home
- remember that personal relationships have to be nurtured. Never take your partner for granted. If you do, he or she might not be there one day when you return from work, three hours late, for the third time in a week.

FINDING TIME FOR THE CHILDREN

It is very important indeed to consider your children when you return to work. They are likely to be the most affected by your decision, especially if they have been used to Mum or Dad being at home all their lives so far.

If you handle it well, however, children are very adaptable. Explain to them why you are returning to work. To earn some money is probably the most common reason, and one that children will usually accept quite happily. If you tell them that the extra money will buy their next pair of trainers, or pay for them to go to a theme park, you will probably be backing a winner from the start.

The hardest reason to explain is when you are returning to work purely for your own satisfaction. In that instance the children can easily feel that they are not important to you any more, and great care needs to be exercised when explaining the situation to them. Be honest, but be kind as well. Tell them that they do mean just as much to you, but you feel you need an interest outside the home, and that you think working will make you a more patient and better mother/father to them.

Whatever your reason for returning to work, it is very important that you set aside some of your free time to spend with your children. It is up to you to prove to them that you can be a better parent and give them even more attention than before, perhaps spending more concentrated periods of time with them. Finding that time might be a problem at first, but with careful planning you will soon sort out a routine and the children will come to know that certain days and times are for them alone.

If you have children, you should consider the following points **before** you accept the offer of a job:

- Make sure you will have adequate cover for them if they are ill.

- Work out what you are going to do about school holidays and who will be there when they return from school.

- Talk to your children and judge their reactions.

- Involve them in your job choice and the hours you will be working.

- Be prepared for tantrums from younger children for the first few weeks. Try to arrange for a relative to be available to step in if necessary.

- Plan special treats and outings and tell them that these extras are only possible because you are working.

Above all, never put a job before your children. They and your partner should form the most important part of your life. Your children depend on you and your partner for their wellbeing and it is up to you both not to let them down. You must always consider their feelings too. They may be young, but they do have real fears and worries just the same as you.

COPING IF THEY ALL TURN AGAINST YOU

Your partner is moaning *again*. His shirts have not been ironed, supper was due an hour ago, and you forgot to ask about his bad cold. The two children refuse to be left with the childminder. You have reached the end of your tether and begin to wonder if it is all worth it.

Well, having got as far as starting work again, do not be too quick to give it up. They will probably get used to the idea in time and you have got to expect some opposition at the beginning.

Frequently used tear-jerking phrases include:

'You don't love me any more.'
'Your job is more important than I am.'
'How will we manage without you?'
'Please don't leave me Mummy.'

The first fact of life for you to consider is that whatever they all say, you are not indispensable. They can, and probably will, cope without you given time, but do not expect an easy ride. You will, no doubt, be feeling guilty about working anyway if young children are involved, but you must not let them see your guilt feelings. Instead, be firm and state, as many times as necessary, that you *are* going to work, and that you will still find time and love for them as well.

If young children prove to be very upset at being left with an 'outsider' like a childminder, see if someone they are familiar with, such as a close relative, will look after them for a short time, so that they can get used to the idea of you not being there. If, on the other hand, they still seem very upset after a few weeks, and school work or their physical health is suffering, then you really need to consider whether you should be working yet. Perhaps it would be better to stay at home for a little while longer and then try again. But do not give in too easily!

Everyone handles their partner and children in a different way when they return to work, but the most important point to remember is that they should still feel wanted by you.

ASKING FOR THE FAMILY'S HELP

Without a doubt you will not be able to do as much around the house, and it is a good idea to make this clear to everybody from the start. Play on your partner's and/or your children's better nature and ask for their help. Say you are finding it hard to cope with everything and ask if they would be prepared to give you a hand with the day to day chores.

The best way to get help from the family is to work out a rota. If everyone has their own domain and responsibilities then you stand far more chance of getting the work done. Try to vary the rota from week to week and show children, whenever necessary, how to carry out a particular task, rather than expecting them to know without instruction.

Give praise when a job has been done well and do not be too quick to criticise. Perhaps the bathroom has not been cleaned to your exacting standards, maybe the chairs have been arranged in the wrong positions, but does it really matter? As long as everyone is trying their best then accept the help gratefully, and stop looking too closely at the standards achieved.

ARRANGING FAMILY HOLIDAYS TOGETHER

One big advantage of a return to work is that your family is likely to benefit from an injection of extra money coming into the household. It is a good idea to put some of this money aside, if at all possible, to pay for a good holiday at least once a year.

First of all, plan well ahead and make sure that everyone is available to go on holiday at the same time. If you need to keep your children away from school, obtain permission from their headteacher. Next, collect brochures and get the whole family involved in planning where to go. Try to make the holiday a special one, to compensate for the upheaval they will have suffered as a result of your new working life.

Once a decision has been made and the holiday booked, see if you can think of a project for the children to work on in connection with the holiday. For instance, if you are planning a trip to Brittany in France, get them books from the library to read about the area, and, unless they are very young, ask them to learn a few useful phrases that you can all use when you are there.

When you do go on the holiday, concentrate on relaxing and enjoying the togetherness of family life. Leave work worries at work, and give your attention to making sure that you and your family are having a great time.

CASE STUDIES

Sue

Sue is having problems with her new boyfriend, Mike. He wants them to spend more time together. He is not, however, keen on children and Sue insists that her children and time spent with them are very important to her.

One Sunday they do all go out together for a picnic. Sue's youngest child, Sheri, seems upset and will not talk to Mike at all. The following day Sheri refuses to go to school and says that her Mummy is cruel to go to work and leave her. Sue is understandably upset at this sudden turn of events. She talks Sheri round and leaves her at school, but she worries all day and is really anxious by the time she meets her that afternoon.

Sheri continues to be a problem, particularly when Mike is around. Much as she enjoys Mike's company Sue decides that her daughter's wellbeing must come first and she tells Mike that she will not see him any more.

Miraculously Sheri becomes her old self again and tells Sue that she really does not mind her working at all, especially as Sue has promised to buy her a very expensive dolls house for Christmas out of the money she earns.

Sue realises that for the time being her children must come first. Her job is important to her too, but she knows her main responsibility is her children, especially as she is a single parent. Once all the traumas are out of the way she begins to settle into a routine that suits them all, and in July they go on a holiday to the Isle of Wight, which is the first holiday she and the children have had for three years.

Mary

Mary's husband is utterly sick of hearing about Lowprices. His wife relates all the happenings of the day over and over again, at tea time, during the evening and, often, again in bed.

One day he explodes and says he cannot stand any more supermarket talk. Mary is shocked that he has lost his temper and immediately apologises to him, although she is still wondering what has caused such an outburst. When she thinks about it more seriously, however, she realises that she has become something of a bore and she resolves to cut down her chatter about work to an absolute minimum. From then on their relationship improves once more and both of them are pleased that the air has been cleared.

Richard

Richard starts to work late several nights a week to earn some extra money. At first he does not notice the difference in his girlfriend, but gradually she becomes more and more moody and he is forced to ask her what is wrong. She says that she hardly sees him and that both she and their daughter would rather have him at home each evening even if it does mean less money to spend. He says that he has only been working the extra time to provide things for them, but he promises to cut down on the hours in the future.

They only afford a holiday in Blackpool that year, rather than the USA as Richard had hoped, but at least by the time they go his girl-friend and daughter seem a lot happier. He understands now that money does not buy happiness, but the novelty of earning lots of money legit-imately is hard to get out of his system.

Andrew

Andrew has decided he wants to get married. He has asked his girl-friend, but unfortunately she has said no. He is not sure why and keeps pressing her to find out the truth.

It transpires that she is fed up with being told how badly he is treated at work and how lucky she is that he is still doing the job at all. She thinks, quite rightly, that he has a chip on his shoulder and over the last few months she has found him absolutely impossible to live with. She works too, and considers that she contributes just as much as he does to their everyday life.

When she eventually explains all this to him, Andrew knows that she is right. He hates the job so much that he decides to leave and look for something else. This means that the wedding will have to be delayed, but next time he asks he hopes she will feel ready to say 'yes'.

John

John has worried about his teaching standards dropping if he takes on more work. On the other hand, he has a long waiting list and tries to start everyone as soon as he can.

He soon realises, however, that it is not just his teaching standards that will suffer if he takes more students. His children will suffer too as he will not have as much time to spend with them.

Knowing how important his children are to him, John turns down any work that he knows he cannot cope with within the hours he has set aside for his business life.

Paula

Paula and her husband are still doing battle about the amount of time she spends at the Home. Paula does not seem to be able to consider anyone else other than herself. She spends little or no time with her son, and only the occasional evening with her husband.

One evening Paula's husband tells her that he has had enough. Either she changes or she can move in to her precious Home and their marriage will be effectively over. He tells her that he is quite willing to look after their son, who is closer to his father anyway.

Paula is devastated. She suddenly realises that what she has taken for granted for many years might not be there for her any more. She cuts her hours down drastically and starts to spend more time with her son and her husband. The Home runs itself very well under Matron's watchful eye and Paula, for the first time, begins to enjoy her family life.

CHECKLIST

- Are you boring your partner with work stories?

- Are your home relationships going well?

- Have you explained your new working life to your children?

- Do you find time to spend with your family?

- Have you asked them for help with the household chores?

- Are you planning a special holiday so that you all have something to look forward to?

- Do you think your family have accepted that you intend to carry on working?

POINTS FOR DISCUSSION

1 If your children are adamant that they do not want you to return to work, would you still do so (assuming that you do not desperately need the money)?

2 Do you think your partner should share the household chores with you if you are both working?

3 If your company asks you to increase your working hours, would you discuss this with your partner before coming to a decision? If yes, what would be the arguments for and against this increase in hours, assuming no children are involved?

14
Achieving Your Ambitions

KNOWING WHAT YOU WANT AND HOW TO GET IT

Once you have been back at work for a while, your thoughts may begin to turn to your long-term aims and ambitions. You may be quite happy with what you have, in the way of a job and your family life, particularly if the hours of work suit you and the people you work with are friendly.

There is nothing wrong with being ambitious, however, as long as you do not allow your ambition to take over your life. If you want to get on, show your employer that you can work under pressure, that you are well motivated and capable, and in time you may well advance to a job with more responsibility. Employers are always on the look out for keen employees and your efforts are unlikely to be missed.

If you work in a specialised field, it is very important for you to keep up to date with current trends. In many cases professional journals, seminars and conferences will help you to do this. Find out all you can about where you work, get to know the staff of all departments and their duties. Take an interest in publicity material, advertising, anything that will give you more of an insight into the organisation as a whole.

IMPROVING YOUR KNOWLEDGE

Just because you have got a job, there is no reason why you cannot continue to learn. Most of us learn something new every single day of our lives, just by listening, watching and speaking to others.

Many organisations offer in-service training courses for their employees. You will normally be paid whilst you train. Do not think that if you are offered a place on one of these courses there is something wrong with the way you are doing your job. It is more likely that you have been earmarked for promotion and the organisation think it worthwhile to train you further for their benefit as well as yours. Take what they offer. It is all good experience and may well help you in the future.

If you are not offered any specialised training by your organisation, you may find that an evening class will help you to gain extra qualifications and confidence. In these days of fierce competition for jobs, the more qualifications you gain the more chance you stand of either promotion or a different position when the time arises.

Never think you are too old to learn. Improving your knowledge can be fun at any age and you will certainly feel a sense of achievement if you manage to gain qualifications that you always felt were far beyond your capabilities.

GOING FOR PROMOTION

Some people find it hard to accept promotion. Others may jump at the chance. A returner may feel that juggling the increased responsibility at work with a precariously balanced home life will prove to be too much. In addition, if the returner is a woman whose promotion would place her in a higher position than her partner, she may worry about him feeling threatened by her increased superiority.

Assuming you are at least mildly ambitious, however, if you are approached by your employer with regard to promotion, first of all find out what the new job entails. Then give the matter serious thought, if possible talking over the details with someone else, such as your partner or family. Only if you feel really confident about what you will be taking on and that the new job will not interfere with your home life, should you accept the promotion being offered to you.

It may happen that your employer does not actually approach you, but you hear about a forthcoming vacancy in your organisation. In this case, there is nothing to stop you saying that you would like to be considered for the position when it becomes vacant. An employer will admire your initiative even if you are not offered the job in the end. You never know, you may be in line for the next promotion as a result.

There may be occasions when you feel your route to promotion is being blocked for some reason. Perhaps you do not get on very well with the person who would promote you, or perhaps there are no prospects of promotion in your present organisation anyway. This can lead to a deep sense of frustration if you are ambitious and want to progress. First of all, see if you can speak to your boss or someone else at work about your long-term aims and ask them whether the situation is likely to change. If the answer is negative then it may be a good idea for you to look around for another job in a different organisation where your talents can be fully utilised.

GIVING THE RIGHT AMOUNT OF COMMITMENT

An organisation will require you to carry out your duties efficiently and also to be reliable, loyal and trustworthy. They will want you to get on with the other staff and to generally join in the workings of the organisation.

It is up to you to show your employer that you are committed to what you are doing, and that he or she can rely upon you at all times. A committed employee is like a pot of gold for employers today. So often they have to put up with poor timekeeping, unsociable habits, shoddy workmanship, rudeness and just plain bad workers. If you are co-operative, eager to learn, committed to your job and your organisation (within limits), then you will go far. The majority of employers will encourage you as much as they possibly can, and this is one area where mature employees score many times over the vast majority of youngsters, who never seem to want to put extra effort into anything.

Never put your job before your family, but try to show commitment to both. In the present competitive job market, if you are not able to show a commitment to your organisation, you may soon find yourself out of a job. Plenty of other people will be around to step into your shoes, so do not take any chances. Should your present employer ask you to leave, it is unlikely that you will be given a satisfactory reference either, and without a good reference another job will be almost impossible to find. If, however, you do your job to the best of your ability, your employer should have no grounds for complaint.

REFLECTING ON YOUR DECISION TO RETURN TO WORK

By now you should know whether you made the right decision when you decided to return to work.

Spend a few moments thinking about the changes that decision has made to your everyday life. Do you:

- feel a sense of achievement?
- see yourself as a different person?
- get up each morning feeling happy and fulfilled?
- find it hard to imagine not working now?
- get on better with your children and/or your partner?
- still have further ambitions?

If you have answered 'Yes' to the majority of these questions then you definitely made the right decision. Even if you have a few 'No's, it is early days yet and you have probably not settled into a firm routine.

Those of you who returned to work for financial reasons will, no doubt, be finding the extra money very useful. Perhaps you have managed to pay off a loan, save up for something special or generally raise your standard of living.

Returning to work, as long as you are enjoying what you do, means a boost to your self esteem, increased confidence, and feeling that you too can be a success once more.

Welcome back to the world of work! May you continue to succeed in all that you do in the future.

CASE STUDIES

Charting the progress of our six Case Studies two years on from their return to work.

Sue

Sue has become the secretary at the School. They have been so pleased with her progress that they are quite happy for her to choose her hours and take all the school holidays off.

About six months ago Sue started seeing one of the teachers from the junior school next to Knolls Hill. He is obviously used to children and Sue's girls take to him straight away. They spend much of their free time in each other's company and Sue hopes that in the future they may get together on a more permanent basis.

All in all, Sue has never looked back. She is happier now than ever before and feels that her decision to return to work was quite definitely the right one.

Mary

Life has settled down for Mary and her husband. They spend companionable evenings together, both at home and with friends and their life is really quite pleasant.

Mary has increased her hours at Lowprices and has also been promoted to a supervisor. She is happy at work and happy at home. The years she spent tied to the house seem a long way away and at 54 she feels younger now than she did ten years ago.

Richard

Richard is still working at the same place and is very happy there. He has gradually been given more responsibility and is in line for a big promotion very soon.

Six months ago he and his girlfriend got married and bought a small terraced house close to where he works. They have spent lots of time decorating and furnishing it and Richard feels at last he has proved to everyone that he has put the past behind him and his new life is here to stay.

Andrew

Andrew's fortunes have gone from bad to worse. He left his rep's job and began looking for something else. Unfortunately, however, his work record coupled with his high opinion of himself did not impress any prospective employers and work was not forthcoming.

Now, 18 months later, he is still out of work and has lost his girl-friend too. He began to treat her badly and she walked out.

Andrew decides that the only answer for him is to go abroad again and travel from place to place. He is destined never to settle down and do a proper job. He believes it is everyone else's fault that things have gone wrong rather than his own.

John

John is still working at a steady pace and with the aid of his partner is managing his business and the children very well. The children are that bit older and accept that he is working as well as their mother. What they are beginning to realise even more is that because their parents both work, their standard of living has increased and that means more special treats for everyone!

Returning to work, and self employment in particular, has proved to be a very wise choice for John. He is happy, he likes being his own boss, and enjoys meeting all the different people that he teaches.

Paula

Paula has learnt a lot. She has at long last started to think about her family and what they mean to her. At the same time, she has proved to herself that she can start a successful business.

At first the business dominated her life but now she seems to have achieved a realistic compromise. She has also become more human and has managed to shrug off her stuck-up, cocky image, which was really only a 'front' anyway.

Returning to work has made Paula into a better person. She no longer resents her son for keeping her at home. On the contrary, she loves him dearly and is enjoying seeing him grow up. Her relationship with her husband has improved too. She feels a complete person now, and looks forward to sharing the future with her husband and her son, whilst at the same time retaining her supervisory position at the Home.

CHECKLIST

- Do you know what your long-term aims are?
- Do you know how you are going to fulfil them?
- Are you keeping yourself up to date with recent trends in your field of work?
- Are you willing to go on training courses?
- Do you know about evening classes in your area?
- Would you like to be promoted?
- Are you a loyal and trustworthy employee?
- Did you make the right decision to return to work?
- Has it changed you as a person?

POINTS FOR DISCUSSION

1   What questions would you ask your employer if he or she offers you promotion?

2   List the advantages and disadvantages of
    a)   self employment
    b)   being employed by another person or organisation

3   Write down your dreams and ambitions for the future, both in your working and home life. Look through the list and see how many of your dreams could become reality if you work towards them. Now it is up to you to prove to yourself that you can achieve whatever you set your mind to.

Glossary

Communicate. To give, receive or exchange information with others

Correspondence. Writing of letters, memos, reports, etc

Customer. Person or organisation buying goods or services

Customs and Excise. Department of Civil Service, responsible amongst other things for collecting VAT

Delegate. To give a task to another person

Environment. The surroundings you live and work in

Facsimile. Reproduction of a document via telephone lines

Income tax. Tax payable to the State, via the Inland Revenue, on money earned

Inland Revenue. Body responsible for the administration of our tax laws, including the collection of income tax

Interest. Amount paid on a sum of money borrowed or invested in a bank or building society account

Interview. Formal conversation between two or more people with a specific aim in mind

Invoice. Business document giving details of goods or services supplied with their prices

Keying in. Term used to indicate the use of a keyboard for producing a typewritten copy of a document

Market research. Measures taken to identify and assess a potential market

Memorandum. A note used to pass information between colleagues in the same organisation

Minutes. Notes containing the important points of a meeting

National Insurance. A scheme run by the Government to provide payments to individuals when they are sick or unemployed, as well as the state pension. It is funded with contributions made by employees as a percentage of their income, and also with contributions by employers

National Vocational Qualifications. New practical qualifications based on standards — all approved by industry and commerce — against which the ability to do a job is measured

Objectives. Targets or goals to be achieved

Personal hygiene. Taking care of appearance and cleanliness

Redundancy. When an employee is no longer required to work for an organisation. In some cases redundancy money is paid

Relevant. Applicable to the subject

Returners. Term used for those people who have, for some reason, taken a break from work and are now returning to the workplace

Skills. Practical expertise needed to do a particular job

Teletext. Public television systems such as Ceefax, Oracle etc, consisting of pages and pages of information on a variety of subjects such as news, travel, weather, gardening, sport

Turnover. Total value of goods or services sold in a set time, which is usually one year

Useful Addresses

National Association for the Care and Resettlement of Offenders (NACRO), National Education Advisory Service, 567A Barlow Moor Road, Manchester M21 2AE. Provides information and advice on colleges, courses and grants for ex-prisoners.

National Council for One Parent Families, 255 Kentish Town Road, London NW5 2LX. Offers information and guidance to one parent families, including a book entitled 'Returning to Work — a guide for lone parents', price £3.50.

National Council for Vocational Qualifications, 222 Euston Road, London NW1 2BZ. Offers information on the wide range of recently introduced National Vocational Qualifications (NVQs).

Open University, Central Enquiries, PO Box 200, Milton Keynes, MK7 6YZ. Offers degree, diploma and certificate courses, open to all adults, regardless of their present qualifications.

Skill: National Bureau for Students with Disabilities, 336 Brixton Road, London SW9 7AA. Develops opportunities for training and employment for those with disabilities or learning difficulties.

The Open College, Freepost, Warrington WA2 7BR. Provides work-related courses for those who want to study at home.

Women Returner's Network, 8 John Adam Street, London WC2N 6EZ. Works with industry, commerce and educational organisations to make women's re-entry into the working world easier.

Further Reading

Making a Comeback, Margaret Korving (Business Books Ltd)
Returning to Work, Alex Reed (Kogan Page)
Back to Work, Gemma O'Connor (Optima)
Women Going Back to Work, Frankie McGowan (N & P Publishing)
Going Freelance, Geoffrey Golzen (Kogan Page)
Working for Yourself without Capital, B H Elvy (The Macmillan Press Ltd)
Collins Office Handbook (HarperCollins Publishers)
How to Work in an Office, Sheila Payne (How To Books Ltd)
How to Apply for a Job, Judith Johnstone (How To Books Ltd)
How to Manage People at Work, John Humphries (How To Books Ltd)
How to Communicate at Work, Ann Dobson (How To Books Ltd)
How to Get that Job, Joan Fletcher (How To Books Ltd)
How to Pass that Interview, Judith Johnstone (How To Books Ltd)
How to Raise Business Finance, Peter Ibbetson (How To Books Ltd)
How to Start a Business from Home, Graham Jones (How To Books Ltd)

Index